Praise for *The Cargo Rebellion: Those Who Chose Freedom*

"Three cheers for this creative graphic history from below! The mighty mutiny of four hundred Asian workers aboard the ship *Robert Bowne* is told here with verve and visual power, showing how the violence of global capitalism met resolute resistance. Read and be inspired by this timeless and heroic tale."
—Marcus Rediker, cocreator of *Prophet against Empire: Benjamin Lay, a Graphic Novel*

"'We chose to remember.' Through deft writing and powerful illustrations, Benjamin Barson, Jason Oliver Chang, Alexis Dudden, and Kim Inthavong draw our attention to Chinese rebellion, a mutiny of four hundred Chinese indentured men to secure freedom from captivity. Their insistence on remembering dislodges us from a collective amnesia that erases histories of Asian resistance. This is a story needed now more than ever to connect violence against Asian Americans to the workings of global racial capitalism and ongoing enslavements in the present."
—Diane Fujino, editor of *Contemporary Asian American Activism: Building Movements for Liberation*

"*The Cargo Rebellion: Those Who Chose Freedom* is an eloquently written and beautifully illustrated account of a landmark incident of successful resistance and rebellion by nineteenth-century indentured Chinese workers. It relates a story that has been hidden from official histories but endures in the countermemories of freedom-loving people. Today, when new virulent and violent forms of racial capitalism use displacement, dispossession, and deportation to consign working people to increasingly unlivable destinies, *The Cargo Rebellion* provides a model of the irrepressible power of the people that is well worthy of admiration and emulation."
—George Lipsitz, author of *The Possessive Investment in Whiteness*

"If we are to defeat the evils of globalization, we must make it our duty to unearth the lost histories of workers, refusers, and rebels—especially those who have been moved, en masse, against their will, around the globe and across the oceans in the service of capitalist accumulation. *The Cargo Rebellion* moves a heavy history in just twenty-eight exquisite pages. It's an invitation to remember. An ode to an audacious workers' struggle on the high seas. And to salute those who refused to work on an island of shit."
—Kanya D'Almeida, author of "I Cleaned the —," winner of the 2021 Commonwealth Short Story Prize

"*The Cargo Rebellion* is a brilliant fusion of arts depicting a global working-class struggle, long ago, for the precious hope of freedom."
—Paul Buhle, coeditor of *Encyclopedia of the American Left*, authorized biographer of C.L.R. James

"*Cargo* carries a precious load. Long live the Afro-Asian legacy to liberation!"
—Quincy Saul, author of *Maroon Comix: Origins and Destinies*

"This strikingly illustrated work recounts a very powerful and inspiring story of resistance to Western imperialism and capitalist exploitation. It is a notable chapter in the struggle between domination and liberation that must not be forgotten. Perhaps even more importantly, it is the kind of story that kindles our righteous indignation and strengthens our will to continue that struggle today."
—John P. Clark, author of *Between Earth and Empire* and *The Impossible Community*

THE
CARGO
REBELLION

THE CARGO REBELLION

THOSE WHO CHOSE FREEDOM

Jason Chang · Benjamin Barson · Alexis Dudden
Illustrated by Kim Inthavong

2023

WRITTEN BY
Jason Oliver Chang, Benjamin Barson, and Alexis Dudden

BASED ON THE RESEARCH OF
Alexis Dudden

ILLUSTRATED BY
Kim Inthavong

LAYOUT & EDITING
Adam Cooper-Terán

PRODUCED BY
Jason Oliver Chang

THANKS TO THE GENEROUS FUNDING OF
UConn Provost Carl Lejuez

OPPORTUNITY FUND

Generous support for this project was provided from the Opportunity Fund based in Pittsburgh, PA.

UCONN AAASI

We thank the following at the University of Connecticut for generous publication support:
Asian and Asian American Studies Institute
College of Liberal Arts and Studies Dean's Office
Department of History
Office of the Provost
University of Connecticut Humanities Institute

The Cargo Rebellion: Those Who Chose Freedom
Jason Chang, Benjamin Barson, Alexis Dudden, and Kim Inthavong © 2023
This edition © PM Press

ISBN (hardcover): 978-1-629-63964-2
ISBN (ebook): 978-1-629-63979-6
LCCN: 2022950914

10 9 8 7 6 5 4 3 2 1

Printed in the USA

DEDICATED TO
ROGER N. BUCKLEY
1937–2020

HOW MANY WHO FOUGHT AGAINST
INDENTURE AND BONDAGE

ARE BURIED AT SEA?

NOT ALL WHO REBEL ARE REMEMBERED.

THE STORY OF THE *ROBERT BOWNE* MUTINY
SHOWS THE STRUGGLE OF INDENTURED CHINESE MEN AGAINST
AMERICAN CAPITALISM AND A GLOBAL ECONOMY
WHICH PROFITED FROM THEIR DEATH AND EXPENDABILITY.

THE SEA IS VAST AND CARES NOT FOR HUMANITY.

HOWEVER, WE ARE CONNECTED, NOT BY BLOOD, BUT BY **THIS** WATER
—AND **WE** CHOOSE TO REMEMBER.

245 COOLIES MUTINIED ABOARD CAPTAIN JEAN PAINE'S FRENCH SHIP *ALBERT* IN 1850
352 COOLIES MUTINIED ABOARD CAPTAIN W.L. MULLIN'S BRITISH SHIP *VICTORY* IN 1851
546 COOLIES MUTINIED ABOARD CAPTAIN HARRIS'S BRITISH SHIP *BRITISH SOVEREIGN* IN 1852
400 COOLIES MUTINIED ABOARD CAPTAIN BRYSON'S U.S. SHIP *ROBERT BOWNE* IN 1852
410 COOLIES MUTINIED ABOARD THE PORTUGUESE SHIP *ADAMASTOR* IN 1853
350 COOLIES MUTINIED ABOARD CAPTAIN HYMANA'S DUTCH SHIP *BANCA* IN 1856
240 COOLIES MUTINIED ABOARD CAPTAIN CARIGNAG'S FRENCH SHIP *ANAISE* IN 1857
850 COOLIES MUTINIED ABOARD CAPTAIN JOHNSON'S U.S. SHIP *FLORA TEMPLE* IN 1859
365 COOLIES MUTINIED ABOARD THE CHILEAN SHIP *GREYHOUND* IN 1860
588 COOLIES MUTINIED ABOARD THE SPANISH SHIP *ENCARNACIÓN* IN 1861
715 COOLIES MUTINIED ABOARD THE FRENCH SHIP *CAROLINE* IN 1865
906 COOLIES MUTINIED ABOARD CAPTAIN GIRAUD'S FRENCH SHIP *EUGENE ADELLE* IN 1866
462 COOLIES MUTINIED ABOARD CAPTAIN CHAPPOT'S FRENCH SHIP *BANGKOK* IN 1867
720 COOLIES MUTINIED ABOARD THE PERUVIAN SHIP *CAYALTI* IN 1868
531 COOLIES MUTINIED ABOARD CAPTAIN RANEE'S FRENCH SHIP *TAMARIS* IN 1869
381 COOLIES MUTINIED ABOARD CAPTAIN NICALSE'S BELGIAN SHIP *FREDERICK* IN 1870
655 COOLIES MUTINIED ABOARD CAPTAIN GARAY'S PERUVIAN SHIP *DON JUAN* IN 1871
535 COOLIES MUTINIED ABOARD CAPTAIN HUE'S FRENCH SHIP *JACQUES SEURIN* IN 1872

TRANSATLANTIC SLAVERY FUELED GLOBAL COMMERCE FOR CENTURIES, CREATING ENORMOUS WEALTH AND GEOGRAPHIES OF BRUTALITY ACROSS THE AMERICAS, WHERE THE LIVES OF THE ENSLAVED OFTEN ENDED WITHIN 10 TO 15 YEARS AFTER FORCIBLE TRANSFER TO THE NEW WORLD.

BY THE 1830S MORE THAN TWO MILLION ENSLAVED AFRICANS LIVED IN THE U.S. SEVERAL EVENTS HELPED MAKE ENSLAVEMENT OF AFRICANS TOO POLITICALLY COSTLY. FIRST, ***THE HAITIAN REVOLUTION,*** ENDING IN 1804, IN WHICH MORE THAN 100,000 ENSLAVED PEOPLE ROSE UP AGAINST THEIR MASTERS AND CLAIMED THE ISLAND FOR THEMSELVES.

LATER, IN 1839, THE ***AMISTAD*** MUTINY HELPED ILLUSTRATE THE BRUTALITY OF HUMAN CARGO AND THE ONGOING SUFFERING OF ENSLAVED PEOPLE, EVEN THOUGH THE SLAVE TRADE HAD BEEN OUTLAWED IN THE U.S. IN 1808.

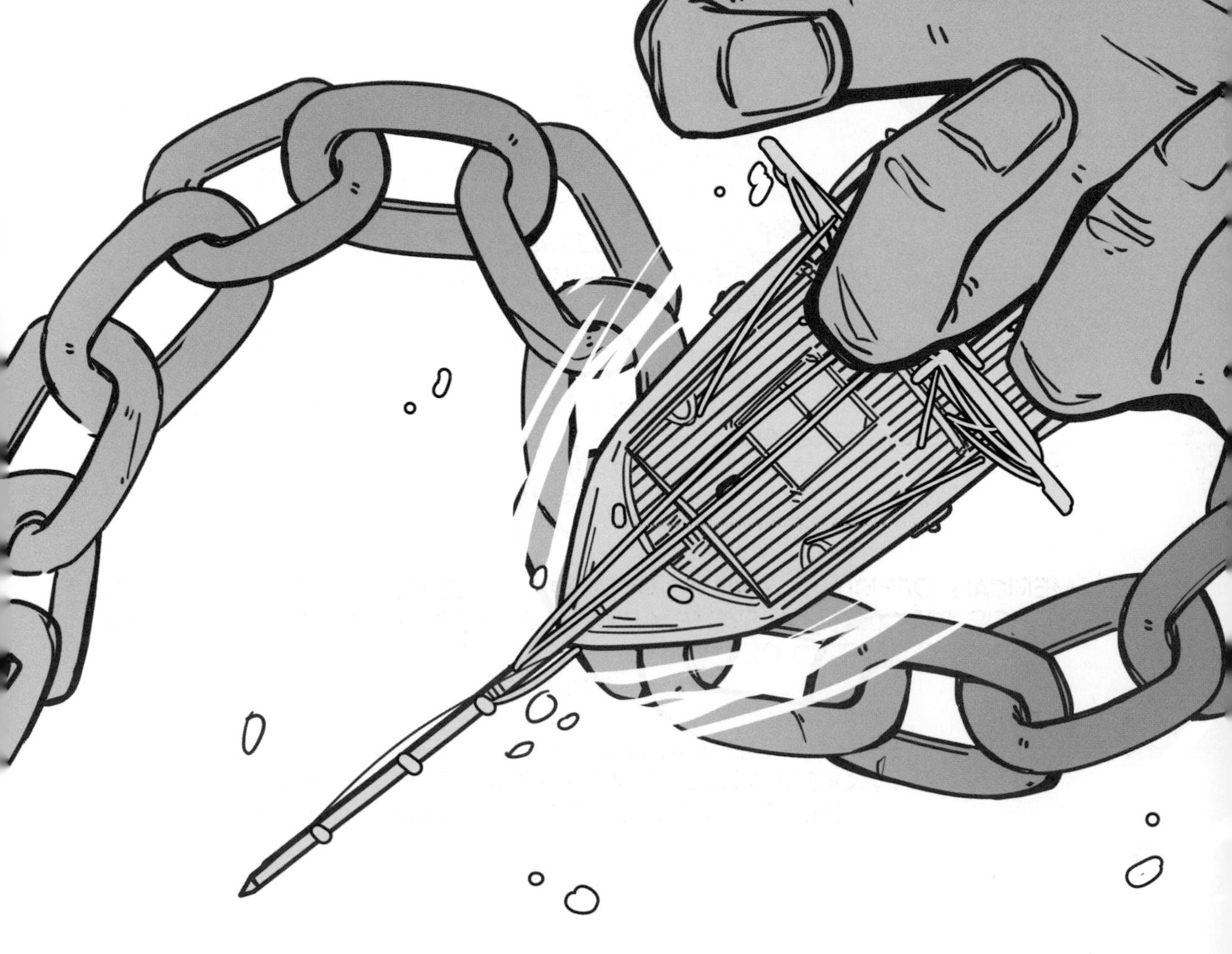

A CARGO OF AFRICANS COMMITTED MUTINY ON THE SPANISH SHIP *LA AMISTAD*, EN ROUTE TO CUBA. THE SHIP WAS APPREHENDED OFF *LONG ISLAND*. MUTINEERS WERE HELD IN *NEW HAVEN, CT.*

JUDICIAL PROCEEDINGS CENTERED ON THE STATUS OF PEOPLE AS PROPERTY. THE COURT SIDED WITH *SENGBE PIEH*, SIGNALING A CHANGE IN U.S. ATTITUDES. ALTHOUGH A MILE MARKER IN THE STRUGGLE FOR ABOLITION, *U.S. V. LA AMISTAD* WAS NOT THE FINAL WORD.

AMERICAN OFFICIALS AND PLANTATION INTERESTS WORRIED ABOUT HOW THEIR AGRICULTURAL SYSTEM WOULD SURVIVE WITHOUT THEIR HUMAN PROPERTY. IN THIS QUANDARY, AMERICANS TURNED TO THE BRITISH INDENTURE SYSTEM OF THE PACIFIC.

WHILE *LA AMISTAD'S* MUTINEERS WON, A STRIKINGLY SIMILAR QUESTION WOULD ARISE 13 YEARS LATER IN THE PACIFIC WITH CHINESE PEOPLE AS CARGO WHO CHOSE TO REBEL.

THE PLANTATION OWNERS AROUND THE WORLD WERE IN DIRE NEED FOR EXPLOITABLE LABOR AS THE BRITISH ABOLISHED THEIR SLAVE TRADE IN 1833. COOLIES WERE TRANSPORTED TO PLANTATIONS ACROSS THE PACIFIC AND ATLANTIC WORLDS, INCLUDING THE U.S. HUNDREDS OF AMERICANS WERE INVOLVED IN THE COOLIE TRADE AS IT FUELED THEIR OVERSEAS BUSINESSES AND INTENSIFIED THE INDUSTRIALIZATION OF AN EXPANDING AMERICAN CAPITALIST EMPIRE.

THE SO-CALLED COOLIE TRADE WAS A MASSIVE INTERNATIONAL PIPELINE TO TRANSPORT HUNDREDS OF THOUSANDS OF CHINESE AND SOUTH ASIANS WHO WERE CONTRACTED AS INDENTURED SERVANTS IN EXCHANGE FOR WAGES. EVEN THOUGH THEY SIGNED CONTRACTS, THESE WERE OFTEN BROKEN BY UNSCRUPULOUS CAPTAINS.

MANY CHINESE COOLIES WERE MORE OR LESS FORCED INTO THESE CONTRACTS DUE TO OUTSTANDING DEBT AND KIDNAPPING. THE FIRST *OPIUM WAR (1839-1842)*, WAGED BY THE BRITISH NAVY, FORCED CHINA TO PERMIT THE MASSIVE IMPORTATION OF OPIUM INTO CHINA AND CEDED HONG KONG TO BRITISH RULE. IT ALSO LEGITIMIZED THE COOLIE TRADE.

COOLIE LABOR CONTRACTED IN *XIAMEN* HAD MANY DESTINATIONS: *CUBA, PANAMA, LOUISIANA, HAWAII, BRITISH GUIANA, CALIFORNIA*. THE MOST FEARED LOCATION WAS *THE CHINCHA ISLANDS* IN PERU.

FOR THOUSANDS OF YEARS THE EXCREMENT FROM SEA BIRDS PILED UP ON THOSE ISLANDS, PRODUCING AN EXTREMELY VALUABLE AGRICULTURAL FERTILIZER KNOWN AS GUANO. IT WAS AS VALUABLE AS IT WAS DANGEROUS. THE AMMONIA CLOUDS PRODUCED BY THIS BIRD DUNG KILLED TENS OF THOUSANDS OF WORKERS, AND MORE THAN TWO-THIRDS DIED.

PERU

Isla Norte Chincha

Isla Centro Chincha

Isla Sur Chincha

THE YEAR: 1852. A CONNECTICUT BUSINESSMAN BY THE NAME OF LESLIE BRYSON SETS OUT WITH HIS SHIP THE **ROBERT BOWNE.**

HIS DESTINATION: **AMOY,** KNOWN TODAY AS **XIAMEN, CHINA.** HE MADE THE JOURNEY NOT TO SEEK FAME OR FORTUNE, NOR TO START A NEW LIFE, BUT TO SEEK A VERY SPECIFIC BOUNTY: THE PROFITS OF SHIPPING 400 CHINESE "COOLIE" LABORERS.

CHINA

XIAMEN

THE LABORERS CONTRACTED BY BRYSON WERE TOLD THEY WOULD BE GOING TO **SAN FRANCISCO**.

AS DAYS PASSED, RUMORS SPREAD ON THE BOAT THAT BRYSON WAS LYING, THAT THEIR REAL DESTINATION WAS THE DREADED CHINCHA ISLANDS. THE 400 WORKERS MADE A PACT: THEY WOULD NOT BE TAKEN THERE —**BY ANY MEANS NECESSARY.**

ONE DAY, BRYSON CUT OFF THE **QUEUES**, OR BRAIDED HAIR, OF THE WORKERS TO BREAK THEIR SPIRITS —AND THIS WAS A TIPPING POINT, AS IT BROKE CHINESE IMPERIAL LAW. THE LABORERS ROSE UP AND KILLED CAPTAIN BRYSON.

THE MUTINEERS ATTEMPTED TO SAIL BACK TO CHINA ...

BUT THEIR BOAT HIT A CORAL REEF NEAR *ISHIGAKI ISLAND* IN THE EAST CHINA SEA, PART OF THE RYUKYU KINGDOM AND CLOSER TO CHINA THAN JAPAN.

THEY WERE FORCED TO BEACH IN THE *YAEYAMA ISLANDS*.

MUTINEERS WHO SURVIVED THE SWIM ASHORE HAD TO CONTEND WITH POISONOUS SNAKES AND EVENTUALLY BEING HUNTED BY BRITISH FORCES SET ON APPREHENDING THEM.

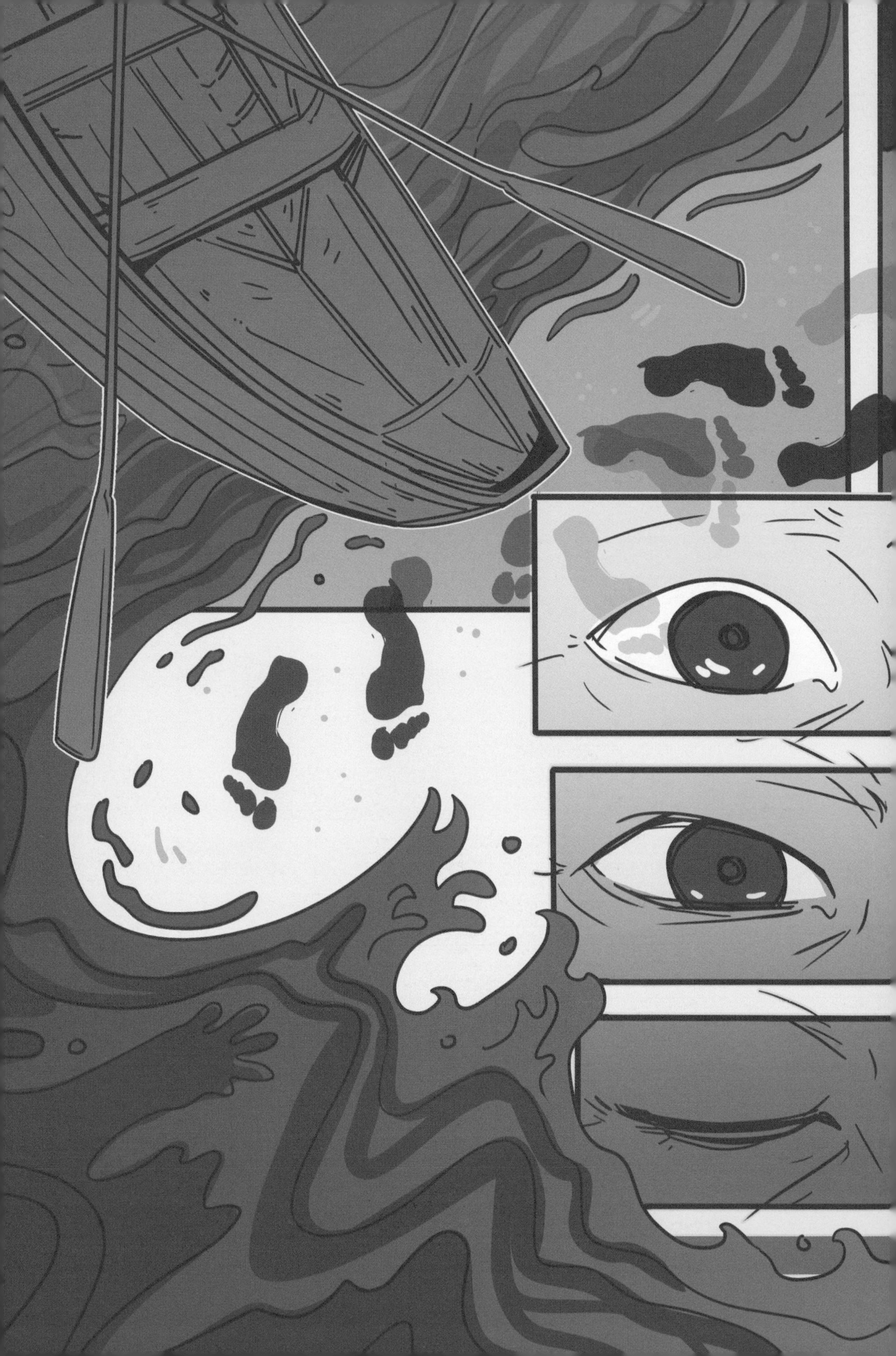

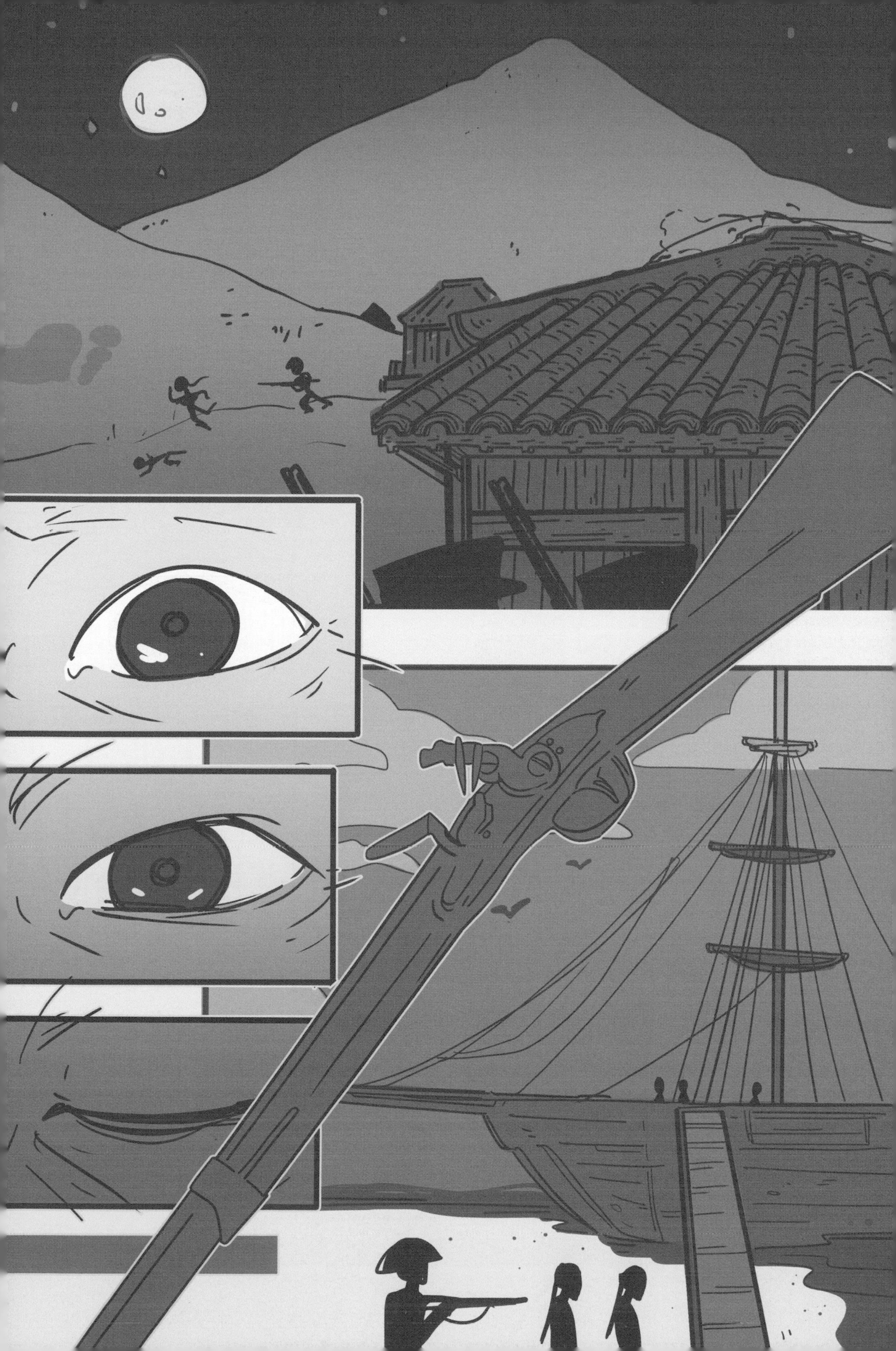

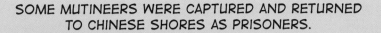

SOME MUTINEERS WERE CAPTURED AND RETURNED TO CHINESE SHORES AS PRISONERS.

Bryson was Killed by his Laborers!

THE INCIDENT IMMEDIATELY ATTRACTED THE ATTENTION OF THE UNITED STATES, WHO WANTED THE MUTINEERS TRIED FOR PIRACY. U.S. OFFICIALS PINNED THEIR LEGAL CLAIMS ON THE LAW OF THE SEA ESTABLISHED EARLIER IN 1836, ASSUMING THAT QING OFFICIALS WOULD PLAINLY SEE THE COOLIES AS THE CRIMINALS IN THIS CASE.

Are the Coolies not men like you and I? You have not the authority to enslave these people!

QING OFFICIALS CONTESTED THE AUDACIOUS ASSERTION THAT THE LAW OF THE SEA WAS RELEVANT IN THIS CASE BECAUSE, IN THEIR EYES, THE CRIME TOOK PLACE IN THE QING IMPERIAL COURT'S JURISDICTION. AFTER ALL, IT WAS THE AMERICANS WHO COMMITTED THE INITIAL CRIME OF DECEIT, FORGERY, AND KIDNAPPING.

THE UNUSUAL FEATURE OF THE *ROBERT BOWNE* CASE IS THAT SO MANY SURVIVORS WOUND UP IN DIFFERENT PLACES, REPRESENTING MULTIPLE FACETS OF THE EVENT. AS A RESULT, A NUMBER OF NATIONAL INTERESTS WERE BROUGHT TO LIGHT.

SIMPLY PUT, THE INCIDENT LAUNCHED THE FIRST TRULY MULTINATIONAL MODERN LEGAL DEBATE INVOLVING THE SEAS IN EAST ASIA, CALLING INTO QUESTION NOT JUST THE FATE OF THE SURVIVING MUTINEERS BUT DRAWING INTO COMPETITION AT LEAST FIVE DIFFERENT LEGAL CODES: THOSE OF CHINA'S *QING COURT*, THE *RYUKYU KINGDOM*, JAPAN'S *TOKUGAWA SHOGUNATE*, AND *AMERICAN* AND *BRITISH* INTERESTS.

THE UNITED STATES NEEDED TO MAINTAIN THIS UNREGULATED, INVISIBLE FORM OF SLAVERY. AFRAID OF EXPOSING ITS LACK OF MORAL AND LEGAL STANDING, IT DID NOT PURSUE THE ISSUE FOLLOWING THE INITIAL DEFEAT.

WITH NO JUDICIAL ABILITY TO JUSTIFY PURCHASING HUMAN BEINGS —ILLEGAL BY THAT TIME FOR AMERICAN CITIZENS—AND WITH THE UNITED STATES ALREADY EMBROILED IN THE SECESSIONAL DIFFERENCES THAT WOULD LEAD TO THE CIVIL WAR, BOTH SOUTHERN AND NORTHERN BUSINESSES WANTED TO MAINTAIN THIS SOURCE OF LABOR WITHOUT TOO MANY TOUGH QUESTIONS.

FOR THIS REASON, THE TALE OF THE *ROBERT BOWNE* DID NOT BECOME THE *AMISTAD* OF THE PACIFIC. DESPITE THE QING COURT'S VICTORY, STATE-SPONSORED INVOLVEMENT IN HUMAN TRAFFICKING CONTINUED, AND CONTINUES, TO BE FUNDAMENTAL TO THE GLOBAL ECONOMY.

THE COOLIE TRADE WAS OSTENSIBLY OUTLAWED IN 1862, WHEN PRESIDENT LINCOLN SIGNED THE ACT TO PROHIBIT IT. HOWEVER, IT WAS CONTEMPT FOR ASIAN MIGRATION THAT MOTIVATED THE PRESIDENT TO BAN THE COOLIE TRADE FROM THE UNITED STATES.

THE CULTURAL STIGMA LIVED ON. CHINESE WORKERS WERE FOREVER MARKED AS "COOLIES," EVEN AS THEY BECAME GOLD RUSHERS, RAILROAD WORKERS, OR SOJOURNERS.

THIS CONTEMPT INFLUENCES HOW WE REMEMBER—AND FORGET—THIS MOMENT. IN NEW HAVEN, THERE IS NO MEMORIAL TO THE COOLIES WHO LOST THEIR LIVES AT SEA, BUT THERE IS A HEADSTONE TO MARK CAPTAIN BRYSON'S LIFE.

IN 1971, ISHIGAKI RESIDENTS CONSTRUCTED A MEMORIAL TO THE CHINESE LABORERS WHO LOST THEIR LIVES ON THEIR SHORES.

JOIN US IN BUILDING A MOVEMENT...

RACIAL CAPITALISM CONTINUOUSLY CREATES THE DEMAND FOR TRAFFICKING HUMAN LABOR AS WELL AS THE CONDITIONS FOR FORGETTING THEIR STRUGGLE, ENSURING THAT ANOTHER GROUP WILL FALL INTO DESPERATION OR OUT OF VISIBILITY TO BECOME CAPITALISM'S NEXT SOLUTION. THE LEGACIES OF COOLIE LABOR HAVE NOT LEFT US.

IN 1995, IN EL MONTE, CALIFORNIA, 72 THAI WORKERS WERE FOUND ENSLAVED IN THE GARMENT INDUSTRY.

ACCORDING TO A 2016 REPORT FROM THE *UN OFFICE ON DRUGS AND CRIME,* MORE THAN FOUR MILLION WOMEN AND GIRLS WERE SOLD INTO SEX TRAFFICKING SCHEMES—70% WERE FROM ASIA.

THE STRUGGLE FOR A TRULY EMANCIPATED FUTURE BEGINS WITH THE STRUGGLE AGAINST RACIAL CAPITALISM. TOGETHER, WE CAN STRIVE FOR A GLOBAL ETHICS OF DE-OBJECTIFICATION.

BUT THIS WILL NEVER HAPPEN IF WE LIVE IN A WORLD WHERE HUMAN BEINGS CAN STILL BE CALLED "CARGO."

...WHERE WE CAN ABOLISH HUMAN SLAVERY AND ITS AFTERLIVES

Bibliography

Davids, Jules, ed. *American Diplomatic and Public Papers: The United States and China*. Ser. 1, *The Treaty System and the Taiping Rebellion, 1842–1860*. Vol. 17, *The Coolie Trade and Chinese Emigration*. Wilmington, DE: Scholarly Resources, 1973.

Irick, Robert L. "Ch'ing Policy Toward the Coolie Trade, 1847–1878." Unpublished PhD diss., Harvard University, 1977.

Kuhn, Philip. *Chinese among Others: Emigration in Modern Times*. New York: Rowman and Littlefield, 2008.

Lowe, Lisa. *The Intimacies of Four Continents*. Durham, NC: Duke University Press, 2015.

西里 喜行 (Nishizato Kiko) 苦力貿易とロバート・バウン号事件：福建師範大学にお
けるシンポジウムへの基調報告苦力貿易とロバート・バウン号事件：福建師範大学にお
けるシンポジウムへの基調報告 ("Coolie Trade and the Robert Bowne Mutiny Incident," reports presented to the Symposium in Fujian Teachers University)
琉球大学教育学部紀要 第一部 (Ryukyu University Education Department, 1986)

Wakeman, Frederic. "American Historical Association, Presidential Speech, December 28, 1992." *American Historical Review* 98, vol. 1 (February 1993): 1–17.

Young, Elliott. *Alien Nation: Chinese Migration in the Americas from the Coolie Era through World War II*. Raleigh: University of North Carolina Press, 2014.

WHAT HAPPENS IN HISTORY IS DIFFERENT FROM HOW PEOPLE REMEMBER IT, WHICH HAPPENS IN THINGS LIKE BOOKS, MOVIES, AND SONGS.

THE STORY AT THE HEART OF THIS BOOK—THE **ROBERT BOWNE** REBELLION—IS VISUAL AND VISCERAL AND BEGS TO BE TOLD OUT LOUD, AND THAT'S HOW THE CARGO PROJECT BEGAN.

ARCHIVAL RESEARCH INTO THIS LONE EVENT SPURRED QUESTIONS OF HOW TO MAKE URGENT THE BROADER HISTORY AT ITS CORE: THE EXPLOITATION OF HUNDREDS OF THOUSANDS OF CHINESE AND SOUTHEAST ASIAN WORKERS IN THE COOLIE TRADE.

THANKS FOR READING AND FOR THINKING ABOUT EVERYTHING INVOLVED.

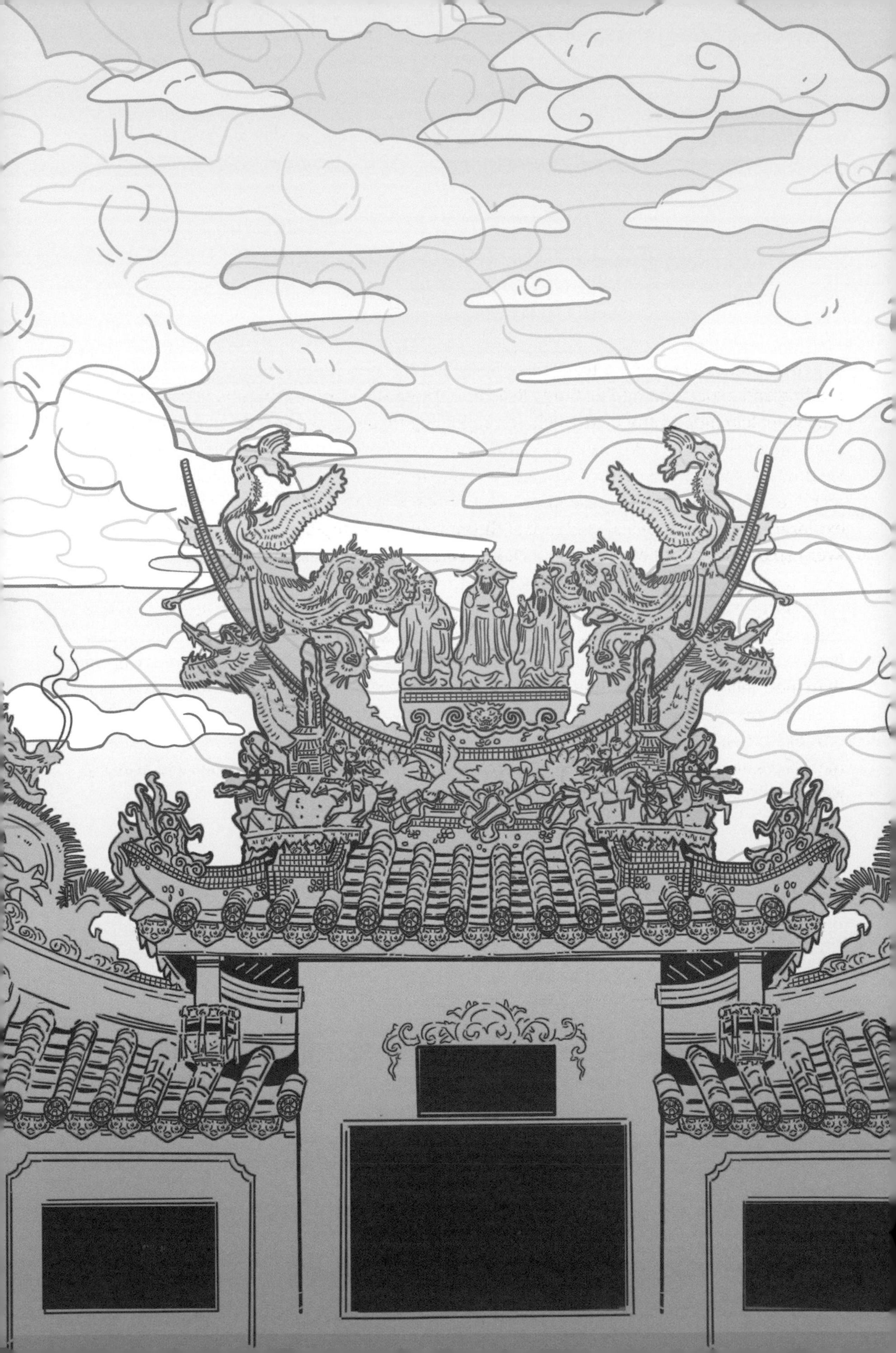

INTERMISSION

Whether you're a student, a teacher, or just plain curious about freedom struggles, after reading and experiencing *The Cargo Rebellion: Those Who Chose Freedom*, you're ready to take your learning to the next level. The following three essays will deepen your understanding of the *Robert Bowne* mutiny, its historical context, and how to teach about this fascinating subject. The essays will also provide more insight into the cultural and political lives of indentured Chinese migrants. Professor Dudden's essay gives you a detailed exploration of the historical evidence of the mutiny and a step-by-step analysis of why this event sparked a global conversation. Next, Professor Chang's essay dwells on the pedagogy of teaching the nineteenth-century trade in indentured Asian workers by detailing an interdisciplinary approach combined with a guided investigation of an interactive data story about the perilous voyages in the times of the *Robert Bowne*. Finally, Dr. Benjamin Barson demonstrates that indentured Chinese workers in the Caribbean and US were more than their labor by showing how the musical traditions they carried with them served as a crucial connection to their African neighbors on plantations and led to shared songs of liberation and the making of the first drum sets. We hope you enjoy these essays and see why the stories of those who chose freedom are precious reminders of the courage and bravery we all possess to make a more just and peaceful world.

The *Robert Bowne* Mutiny
Alexis Dudden

Teaching Asian Indenture
Jason Oliver Chang

From Plantation Percussion to the Sound of Solidarity
Benjamin Barson

THE ROBERT BOWNE MUTINY
ALEXIS DUDDEN

In March 1852, several hundred Chinese laborers—known as coolies—took control of the ship they were on in the East China Sea. They killed the captain of the clipper *Robert Bowne* and several of the ship's officers and mates. This is about the only piece of the *Robert Bowne* mutiny with which its narrators agree.[1]

There are many reasons for encountering different versions of this story. To begin, the protagonists—the mutineers—are forever quoted through other people's words (such as these) because they left no written record of their own. Also significant is that the incident launched the first multinational modern legal debate in East Asia about ocean laws, which involved five competing worldviews (resulting in a lot of words in a lot of languages): the Qing court (China), the Tokugawa shogunate (Japan), Great Britain, the United States, and the Ryukyu Kingdom (Okinawa). In the mix, the Americans and British referred to something new to the others that they maintained made everyone everywhere equally accountable: the international law of the high seas.

Today, a sign at a dragon-laden monument on Ishigaki Island in Japan's southwestern Yaeyama Islands chain states what its sponsors in the 1990s hoped would be remembered: "En route to Taiwan, the ship hit a reef off of Ishigaki. 380 people went ashore." The marker explains that locals took the men to an official residence, where they were kept in a compound. Even now, however, the story does nothing to hide the confusion that ensued, explaining in carved granite that American and British sailors appeared at least three times during the following months and chased the men throughout the island, shooting many to death while dragging others away. Some of the captives who escaped the raids killed themselves in despair; others died of illness after being bitten by the island's deadly vipers; still more drowned trying to swim away from shore.

At the time, some of the islanders made commemorative ceramic bricks to mark the dead, including names, ages, and faraway hometowns. More than a century later, during the 1970s and '80s, local historian Makino Kiyoshi collected as many of these as possible and interred them in lieu of ashes in the dragon-covered *Tojin-baka* (literally, "Chinese grave").

---

1   The primary sources cited for this brief essay are: Jules Davids, ed., *American Diplomatic and Public Papers: The United States and China*, ser. 1, *The Treaty System and the Taiping Rebellion, 1842–1860*, vol. 17, *The Coolie Trade and Chinese Emigration* (Wilmington, DE: Scholarly Resources, 1973); Matsuda Yoshitaka, *Yaeyama Taiwanjin* (Ishigaki, Okinawa: Nanzansha, 2004); Miki Takeshi, *Yaeyama Kenkyu no Rekishi* (Ishigaki, Okinawa: Nanzansha, 2003); John S. Sewall, *The Logbook of the Captain's Clerk*, ed. Arthur Power Dudden (Chicago: R.R. Donnelley and Sons, 1995).

A few are on display in Ishigaki City's wonderful museum of things that have no more important home.[2]

A few people who narrate the *Robert Bowne* story suggest that a rumor about a change in destination triggered the revolt. American consul Peter Parker could show anyone interested the men's signed indenture contracts to work in California. Yet, other accounts would observe that after its departure from Xiamen, word spread quickly aboard ship that Captain Leslie Bryson of New Haven, Connecticut, instead planned to take the men elsewhere, perhaps even to the dreaded Chincha Islands off Peru. Xiamen was known by foreigners as Amoy at the time and was a main exit port for coolie labor to plantations in Cuba, Panama, Hawai'i, British Guiana, California, and several southern US states. The destination most feared among laborers was Chincha, home to thousands of seabirds and unknown to global markets for thousands of years. For mid-nineteenth-century purposes, this remote spot in the eastern Pacific Ocean transformed into one of the planet's richest supplies of guano, prized by fertilizer companies whose owners cared nothing for the mere months it took until the bird dung's ammonia clouds suffocated harvesters to death.

Although the precise location of the *Robert Bowne* mutiny in the East China Sea cannot be known, right away American officials determined that it occurred on the "high seas" and "not within the jurisdiction of China." Two months after the mutiny, on May 21, 1852, American consul Peter Parker wrote to Secretary of State Daniel Webster explaining that although the case could be pursued "strictly speaking . . . under the laws of the United States"—an American citizen had been murdered and American property destroyed on the open ocean—he and other members of the consular delegation determined that it was more "expedient" and likely beneficial to American interests in China to work together with Chinese officials. Referring to Henry Wheaton's 1836 *Elements of International Law* (the main law book of the day), Parker explained that his logic was sensible because China could "punish . . . their subjects agreeably" since the incident had taken place in international territory (i.e., the "high seas"). Parker confirmed his thinking with the commodore of the American fleet, James Aulick: "What expediency dictates in the present instance I conceive as also justified by the law of nations."

By 1852, China's stature as a participant in the "law of nations"—as international law was still most often called—came about through the unequal treaties that the British and Americans and others imposed on the Qing court.[3] The terms of these codes secured extraterritorial privileges for the foreigners, opened ports to international trade, and fixed tariffs—all of which benefited the foreigners defining the laws. Most significant to the *Robert Bowne* mutiny and its aftermath, these treaties—in this case, America's 1844 Treaty of Wanghia—drew China securely into international law's self-referential web, naming

---

2   See Imamura Mitsue and Ishimori Kozue, *Yaeyamajin no Shozo* (Ishigaki, Okinawa: Nanzansha, 2004).

3   See Douglas Howland and Luise S. White, eds., *The State of Sovereignty: Territories, Laws, Populations* (Bloomington: Indiana University Press, 2008).

China at once a member state and an "equal" in the so-called world of nations (万国), yet one already compromised by the hierarchy of European and American interests.

At the time of the mutiny, Peter Parker was American consul in Canton (as Guangzhou was known). John S. Sewall was ship's log keeper aboard the USS *Saratoga*, which would soon lend a hand. He made clear that it was only natural for Parker to believe himself in charge because "our business in China was to protect the interests of American citizens and American commerce in the East." The murder of Captain Bryson was self-evident: Parker learned from surviving crewmen and coolies alike that a number of the Chinese men had slaughtered him; he was also the ship's owner:

> On the port side of the deck lay the captain, stretched full length between the main rigging and the fore part of the cabin, with his head and features covered with blood; the coolies had got hatchets, saws, pikes, and axes, chopping him up in such a way that it would have made any man tremble with horror.

Parker and the American delegation went far beyond murder charges, however. They wanted to make clear that the United States would not tolerate any further act against its citizens and property, and they would accomplish this by arresting and convicting the surviving Chinese men with premeditated "piracy under the law of nations." In their reasoning, they would foreground the "high seas" location of the crime and argue that the offense merited death by execution.

Soon after the initial wave of violence aboard the *Robert Bowne* (somewhere east of Taiwan), the mutineers realized that they did not know how to read charts or sail; then, there were terrible storms. At this point—or before or after—the *Robert Bowne* struck one of Ishigaki Island's many coral reefs and beached. Initially, those aboard did not know where they were. Among the surviving seamen, Robert Bremton, Charles H. Gilberth, William Pendexter, and William Fry later testified that at this juncture they crafted a plan to lighten the ship and free it from the reef, which would at once strand the mutineers and enable the sailors to return to China. They calculated they were to the west and several days to the coast:

> We then got our boat and sampan out, and commenced landing coolies as fast as possible, we think about one hundred that day. . . . Next day, after getting the ship off from the reef, we continued landing the coolies. . . . The coolies then took two of our men on shore; the rest of us then got the long boat out and partly filled her with provisions, in case anything should happen we might take her; the coolies remaining had armed themselves with swords, knives, etc. . . . Friday, continued landing the coolies; we were all taken on shore except the carpenter; they then tried to work the boat for themselves, but they found they could not manage it. Saturday . . . landed most of the coolies; some of us got on board and found only, as we supposed, 15 to 20 coolies on board. . . . We then slipped the cable and made sail on the ship. . . . Next day found 23 coolies on board, and the cook told us that they were plotting to kill us, so we mustered all the arms we could find, called them after and told them we wanted them in the cabin; we put 13 in double rope yarns then, and in the course of the day got the 19 in and fastened, keeping a sentry over them until we reached Amoy.

The unusual thing about the *Robert Bowne* mutiny was not that it happened; at the time, mutinies had, as the American diplomatic historian Jules Davids observed, become "as predictable as the monsoons." Like the famous African slave revolt aboard *La Amistad* in 1839, the rare feature of this history was that so many involved survived it and wound up in so many different places, bringing competing national interests to light.

Ishigaki Island—called "Patchungsan" in official US records, in an Americanized version of its old Chinese name—was determined as the location of hundreds of the accused Chinese. Rounding them up posed a problem seemingly unimaginable today: the United States Navy's Far Eastern Squadron did not have a single ship to spare. The USS *Saratoga* was in Guangzhou, at least ten days' sail away, while at the same time—and to the American diplomats' outrage—the US Navy ordered the pride of the fleet, the USS *Susquehanna* (soon to be differently famous that year, under Commodore Matthew Perry) "to remain" at Hong Kong. The increasingly frenzied American consular officials were compelled yet again to be bested by British dominance and accepted Britain's immediate offer of Her Majesty's ships *Lily* and *Contest* to retrieve the Chinese men left on the island (which was referred to on most charts of the day as part of the "Magicosima" group—today's Miyakojima and "belonging" variously to China or the Ryukyus, and occasionally Japan).

British consul Henry Anthon Jr. described the English sailors' activities to Parker: "*Lily* had taken prisoners some thirty or forty of the coolies, perhaps not so great a number, the remainder escaped over the hills." When the USS *Saratoga* arrived several weeks later, its ship's clerk, John Sewall, found similar terrain, which he would remember with great flourish in his memoirs:

> It proved to be as on the arrival of H.M. brig *Lily*. The birds had flown. The apparition of another avenging fury in the shape of another man-of-war lent wings to their terror, and all but the sick and dying had bolted again for the woods in the wildest helter-skelter of alarm.

Having captured only a fraction of the accused men, several nights later Sewall joined a "second expedition" for coolies on "another midnight prowl like the first." Through torrential rain and thunderstorms, they searched for their "prey" as well as for anyone giving them shelter:

> And by the time we straggled in at the rendezvous site . . . we looked more like a set of shipwrecked pirates ourselves than a company of honest men. . . . All our military ardor was soaked out of us, and a large portion of our morals. . . . The four divisions radiated out into the darkness like the sticks of a fan. . . . It was still a hunt for native cabins. When one was found we silently surrounded it so that nothing could escape and then, suddenly opening the door and thrusting in a lighted torch, we ransacked the hut for hidden pirates. It was not polite, and the gentle inmates were badly frightened.

In the end, Sewall's party came up empty-handed; more than one hundred Chinese eluded the British and the Americans and "had flown to the mountains" and remained on Ishigaki.

Nonetheless, by the middle of June 1852, the Americans decided that they had sufficient evidence to press their case of "piracy upon the high seas." Officials interviewed as many of the survivors as possible—crew and coolie alike—holding preliminary trials for some of the accused aboard nothing less than the USS *Susquehanna* in Hong Kong's harbor, with Commodore Aulick presiding. As far as the Americans were concerned, the Chinese were guilty as charged, and retribution would be soon forthcoming. On June 14, 1852, Peter Parker wrote to the Qing court's high commissioner:

> This act of piracy occurring on board an American vessel, and upon the high seas, the pirates, no matter to what nation they belong, are amenable to the laws of the United States; but, in the present instance, the undersigned, Commodore Aulick, commanding the naval forces of the United States in the China seas, concurring, is willing to waive this right and to deliver over to your excellency the principal offenders to be tried and punished according to the laws of China.

The story, however, takes a sharp turn for the Americans at this point. Within weeks, Parker learned to his surprise—and fury—that the Chinese officials would act not at all as he presumed. On July 9, 1852, the Qing court's high commissioner explained that the "high seas" and "piracy" had nothing to do with anything. The Americans had committed crimes in China against Chinese men; on top of that, the confessions came about under "torture":

> We have examined the case of piracy on board the merchantman "Robert Bowne," and we, the minister and the lieutenant governor, have made a thorough inquiry, and find it to be the style of thing called *buying pigs*. . . . It is unnecessary to multiply discussions upon it.

Having switched matters entirely to the illegal practice of purchasing Chinese for the foreign labor market, the Qing commissioner went further:

> Moreover, in the testimony appended to your dispatch of the 24th ultimo, there was the testimony of Wiley that there were Chinese whose tails had produced insects, (vermin,) and therefore they cut them off, etc., which is still more ludicrous. We have never seen a Chinese, who, on account of vermin, cut off his tail; moreover, by the established laws of China, to cut the tail is the same as to cut off the head, and thus it is manifest the said captain was tyrannical beyond doubt.

American seamen corroborated the assertation that Captain Bryson had ordered the Chinese men's queues chopped off. Some maintained it was for sanitary reasons; the coolies argued it was to demonstrate who was boss.

Ultimately, the American diplomatic papers reveal only Parker's rage at being stalled in his tracks. He makes no mention of the Chinese countercharges in correspondence with Secretary of State Webster. Rather, he repeats the crime of "piracy" and bemoans the Qing officials' "flagrant breach of good faith." He includes copies of correspondence with the Chinese government and explains he will wait "for another opportunity." For its part, the Chinese government's approach to the incident is revealing, because its officials did not challenge America's use of international law as negotiation tool (as they had before and would on numerous occasions through the end of the Qing dynasty in 1911). Instead, Qing officials chose to return the mutiny at sea to a crime on land in such ways that they could assert Chinese control over the situation (no small feat coming so shortly after the first Opium War and in the midst of the first wave of the Taiping Rebellion). They focused their lens on the slave-trading aspect of the coolie labor business—deceit, forgery, kidnapping—and themselves named a notorious Chinese slave trader involved as guilty as charged.

International laws and agreements between foreigners and Chinese at the time prohibited the "buying and selling of pigs"; no US official could turn it into more of a public spectacle, since American nationals were deeply complicit. In ways foreshadowing of contemporary multinational corporate abuse of Chinese labor, by 1852 Americans and others who wanted to do business in China joined the Qing court in decrying slave labor as immoral, agreeing to prohibit its nefarious dealings. At the same time, foreigners would establish and expand their reach along the Chinese coast and expand transport of this illegal cargo all over the world.

The Qing officials' countercharge of coolie slave trading returned the burden of guilt onto American citizens and the United States government. Should American diplomats have pressed further, Secretary of State Daniel Webster would have become directly involved. Only a few years earlier, however, Webster himself had signed the treaty with Britain's Baron Ashburton ending the slave trade on the Atlantic Ocean's "high seas." In a United States of increasing North-South tensions revolving around the triangular African-Atlantic-American slave trade, the China-Pacific-American trade functioned as a lucrative shadow economy for New England and mid-Atlantic businessmen. Who in Washington in the early 1850s would risk introduction of an additional dimension to slave-trafficking debates already imperiling America's national existence?

For reasons ranging from China's assertion of American involvement in forcibly enslaving the accused to what would soon become the United States' overriding concern in the region—Commodore Matthew Perry's "opening" of Japan (1853)—the *Robert Bowne* mutiny disappeared from history despite the efforts of American diplomats in China to make this mutiny into something significant.[4] The forgotten nature of this event, therefore, circles

---

4   In this regard, the *Robert Bowne* insurrection could not have differed more from the *Amistad*, which ended up in the United States Supreme Court after President Martin Van Buren challenged the Connecticut court's decision to free the men and send them home. As to the effect of the mutiny's erasure, John Sewall's memoirs are instructive: "What became of the mutineers? . . . The ringleaders were identified and in due time were forwarded to Canton and turned over to Chinese courts. Perhaps they paid the penalty of their crime. Perhaps their judges, not overfond of foreign barbarians, winked at it as on the whole a meritorious act. We never knew" (Sewall, *Logbook*, 61). Even more noticeably, perhaps, Robert Bowne Minturn (1805–1866)—grandson of the man for whom Captain Bryson's mutinied ship was named, heir to a massive shipping fortune on both maternal and paternal sides, and partner in one of New York's largest shipping houses, Grinnell and Minturn—in 1858 passed through the areas of China and the East China

us back to understanding that in the 1850s the East China Sea remained an "open"—even lawless—"high seas" space whose islands and people were still as ambiguously claimed as the water surrounding them.

As it transpired, Kariwakateikugu Miyara, the Ryukyu Kingdom's official on Ishigaki Island (the former kingdom is now all called Okinawa) would provide the best account. A year after the mutiny, in March 1853, he sent a letter to administrators in Naha on the main Okinawa Island to make clear local Ishigaki displeasure at having to look after the Chinese any longer.[5] In all, 172 men remained stranded on Ishigaki, having survived the British and American raids, and were depleting the native "food supplies." The letter does not specify, yet local women reported being so fearful of the Chinese that they refused to go to the shoreline to dye the fabric used to pay taxes to the Ryukyu king—ostensibly for their protection, which, in turn, the king used to pay portions of his taxes to the Tokugawa system's Satsuma lord as well as to Qing officials. Kariwakateikugu Miyara requested a ship to take the Chinese men home, lest the islanders fall far behind on their "taxes owed." The Ryukyu king consulted with Chinese officials, who determined that the islands were under his control, and two Ryukyu ships returned the men to Fuzhou, which most called home.

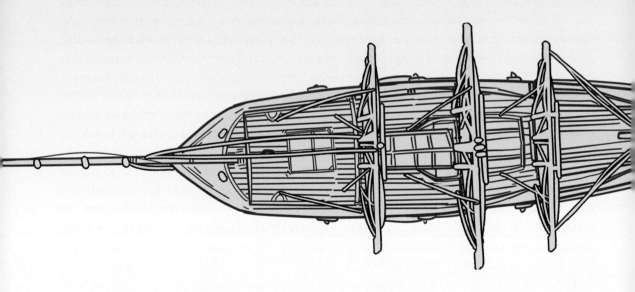

Sea where the 1852 mutiny had taken place. His travelogue is a richly detailed account of what he saw and learned (albeit in the archest possible Orientalist prose), yet he never once mentions the *Robert Bowne* story. See Robert Bowne Minturn, *From New York to Delhi: By Way of Rio de Janeiro, Australia and China* (New York: D. Appleton and Co., 1858).

5   Kariwakateikugu Miyara, *Shomenshu* (Nishihara, Okinawa: University of the Ryukyus, Okinawa Rare Books Collection, Miyara Donchi Collection, March 1853).

TEACHING ASIAN INDENTURE
JASON OLIVER CHANG

In 1836, John Gladstone, a Scotsman and absentee Guianese plantation owner, inquired about the use of contracted laborers from beyond the usual Atlantic indenture circuits and declining trade in enslaved Africans. Drawing from existing contract-labor regimes in South Asia that circulated workers throughout the Indian Ocean, Gladstone made successful contact with Gillanders, Arburthnot and Company in Calcutta and drew up plans to bring one hundred workers to the South American colony to grow and harvest sugar for five to seven years.[1] By 1847, the recruitment and distribution of indentured Asian laborers became institutionalized in British and other European colonial administrations as the so-called "coolie trade." Gladstone's experiment helped initiate a wide-scale labor-migration apparatus that sent hundreds of thousands of South Asian and Chinese contracted laborers to destinations across the globe. This important episode is helping to rewrite Asian American history, because it shows how Asian migration to the Americas had origins in slavery, colonialism, and struggles for freedom. This essay follows my work to bring this change into the classroom. Changing how we teach Asian American history is now more important than ever, since Connecticut and several other states have recently legislated the inclusion of Asian American studies in primary and secondary public education.

Most students and teachers have never heard of the Asian indentured labor system known as the "coolie trade." However, Caribbean Americans are far more familiar with it, because the term *coolie* has survived in their islands' cultures as a derogatory term for a poor Asian person, usually male. In the US context, the term *coolie* fell out of circulation in the 1930s and '40s, when other derogatory terms rose to replace it in connection with US wars, like *Jap* and *gook*. This insulting terminology is unacceptable in usage today, but it is important to be sensitive to the discussion of anachronistic language in learning the truth about the past. Learning about the *Robert Bowne* mutiny teaches how the term *coolie* was used to treat Asian people as disposable workers. In teaching about this, it's important to keep in mind that we instill the lessons of this history and undo the harmful ideology attached to this term. I recommend that students gain familiarity with the term *coolie* but use the term *indentured worker* as a more descriptive and meaningful reference to this community and its history. Teaching Asian American history today means facing our historical silences and dark pasts with honest and accurate accounts so that we can understand more clearly how our present and future are made.

---

1   Gaiutra Bahandur, *Coolie Woman: The Odyssey of Indenture* (Chicago: University of Chicago Press, 2013), 79–80.

The introduction of trans-Pacific labor migration through the trade in indentured Asian workers is a significant, but frequently overlooked, predecessor to the better-known migrations of Chinese families, merchants, miners, farmers, and workers to the US West Coast after the California Gold Rush in 1848. The introductory Asian American history course I inherited at the University of Connecticut bears the title "The Asian American Experience since 1850," reflecting the conception that Asian American history begins with the immigration of Chinese to California in the middle of the nineteenth century. Many other Asian American history courses, indeed broader treatments of US immigration history, replicate the Gold Rush moment to inaugurate the Asian presence in North America. Since Asian American history has many origins, there is no one starting place that is wrong, per se; however, I find it beneficial to unpack the ideological implications of different points of departure. Over the course of the semester, I engage the history of Asian indenture to align Asian American history with the broader region of the hemisphere and the wider history of slavery and colonization in the Americas. I approach the challenge of revising this story for my students by asking them to consider what "coolie" history tells us about the place of Asians in the Americas. By providing my students with a set of primary source materials, I allow them to begin to identify the ways that Asian indenture not only alters the time and space of Asian America but also changes the narrative genres and problems of Asian American history more broadly. This essay chronicles a journey to revise my course by teaching the history of Asian indenture as an introduction to Asian American history. For primary and secondary educators, lessons on Asian indenture are important complements to standard tracks in US history, because they disrupt a black/white binary notion of race as well as tell a more inclusive and accurate story of Asian America.

With recent scholarship as my guide in making changes to the curriculum, I returned to the core concepts of transnationalism, diaspora, and racial formations in Asian American studies. Recent scholars have focused on the Americas, not just the US, to reflect how migration is not bound by the traditional container of the nation, as seen in the work of notable scholars such as Evelyn Hu-DeHart, Erika Lee, Moon-Ho Jung, and Elliot Young, to name a few.[2] "Coolie" history and the larger hemispheric framework are present across the interdisciplines of Asian American studies, and they also catch attention in Latin American studies, as represented by the work of Lisa Yun, Lok Siu, and Kathleen Lopez.[3] Despite these advances in scholarship, teaching resources have not kept pace, although signs of change are present, as exemplified by Erika Lee's widely acclaimed *The Making of Asian America*, a

2   Evelyn Hu-Dehart, "Chinese Coolie Labor in Cuba in the Nineteenth Century: Free Labor of Neoslavery," *Contributions in Black Studies* 12, no. 5 (1994): 38–54; Erika Lee, "Hemispheric Orientalism," *Journal of Asian American Studies* 8, no. 3 (2005): 235–56; Moon-Ho Jung, *Coolies and Cane: Race, Labor, and Sugar in the Age of Emancipation* (Baltimore: John Hopkins University Press, 2009); Elliot Young, *Alien Nation: Chinese Migration in the Americas from the Coolie Era through World War II* (Chapel Hill: University of North Carolina Press, 2014).

3   Lisa Yun, *The Coolie Speaks: Chinese Indentured Laborers and African Slaves in Cuba* (Philadelphia: Temple University Press, 2009); Lok Siu, *Memories of a Future Home: Diasporic Citizenship of Chinese in Panama* (Redwood City, CA: Stanford University Press, 2007); Kathleen Lopez, *Chinese Cubans: A Transnational History* (Chapel Hill: University of North Carolina Press, 2013).

tremendous update to the broad historical survey of Asian American history by pioneers Ronald Takaki and Sucheng Chan.[4]

In Lee's book, Asian American history is situated within the emergence of the modern world, beginning with European plans for an oceanic route to Asia in the sixteenth century and the development of the first trans-Pacific commercial circuits of the Spanish galleon trade between Acapulco, New Spain, and Manila in the Philippines. Lee then directs readers to the global turmoil of the African slave trade and the intensification of industrialization to frame an introduction into the geography, voyages, contexts, and lives of South Asian and Chinese "coolies." Lee writes:

> Just as the roots of Asian immigration to the United States extend back to Europe's search for Asia and the arrival of Asian sailors, slaves, and servants in New Spain, the mass movement of Asian laborers to the United States beginning in the nineteenth century overlaps with and connects to the arrival of Asian coolies in Latin America. Both movements were made possible by the growing European and American presence in Asia and the West's search for labor following the end of African slavery in the Americas. Western slave traders, labor recruiters, steamship companies, missionaries, and officials helped to build the infrastructure that made both unfree Asian migration to parts of Latin America and free Asian migration to North and South America possible. And the idea of the Asian coolie—an unfree laborer who represented a new kind of slavery—would shape Americans' perceptions of Asian immigrants for years to come.[5]

The Making of Asian America makes two critical introductions for the subject of Asian indenture to general readers of Asian American history. First, it shows that indentured-worker diasporas connect US populations of Asians to a broader geography of the Americas and a global history of colonialism and imperialism. Second, it builds an understanding that the US racial figure of the "coolie" was formed on the global stage in response to the decline of the African slave trade. Moon-Ho Jung argues that the ideological figure of the "coolie" was a central crux by which race, labor, and citizenship were transformed in the US at midcentury.[6] Elliot Young contends that what was true for the US, in this regard, was also true for other republics, colonies, and empires in Latin America.[7] In other words, the history of Asian indenture is not just a forgotten chapter, but also a subject that helps to reformulate basic narratives of Asians in American history.

One of the challenges of teaching this subject is that students are not familiar with the narratives that are the object of revision. As a scholar, I might emphasize how the coerced plantation labor of indentured Chinese workers disrupts the typical Gold Rush sojourning narrative of voluntary migrants who faced persecution and were banned and disavowed through the Chinese Exclusion Acts. Yet many students are not aware of the Chinese Exclusion Acts or even a Gold Rush moment. While students may implicitly understand a

---

4   Erika Lee, *The Making of Asian America: A History* (New York: Simon & Schuster, 2016).

5   Lee, *The Making of Asian America*, 35.

6   Jung, *Coolies and Cane*.

7   Young, *Alien Nation*.

generic immigrant narrative as a story of arrival, struggle, and incorporation, the history of these Asian laborers as indentured nonimmigrant workers across the Americas does not fit the common framework of the typical American immigration story. I taught Lee's *The Making of Asian America* for the first time in the spring semester of 2017. After reading the chapter on "coolies," students typically responded to this new narrative in two ways.

On the one hand, some students interpreted anti-"coolie" discourse through the familiar contemporary anti-immigrant trope of "they took our jobs." On the other hand, some students interpreted the history of Asian indenture through what they knew about enslaved Africans. Both interpretations were useful to foment discussion. In an online forum, students addressed the issue of anti-immigrant interpretations of anti-"coolie" discourse and connections to the African slave trade by pointing out from the readings that:

> The Europeans exploited African Americans for the sole purpose of labor, and when they were emancipated, the Europeans exploited Asians next. Europeans were not in competition with the coolies for the domestic jobs. Coolies were specifically placed in field work and hard labor while Europeans were running businesses and shops, working on trades, etc. Plantation work is hard labor that the Europeans forced others who were different from them to perform. There is a clear power dynamic between who runs the plantations and who works in the fields. Coolies and Europeans were never on the same playing field.

Another student responded by writing:

> Europeans and Spaniards did not have to worry about Asians settling in the colonies. Their intention was to use them for backbreaking labor—many would die before they saw the ends of their contracts, and after their working periods were over, they were to return to their homeland. The thought process behind this goes even further than just using Asians as labor mechanisms.

Lee's introduction to "coolie" history helped students to break down the typical immigration model of diaspora, as well as of racial formation, as merely denied belonging.

To deepen my students' understanding, we embarked on a three-week project for them to engage the history of Asian indenture firsthand. I organized this assignment into three parts: comparative readings from primary texts, analysis of data visualizations, and synthetic writing. Rather than focus on what I wanted them to know, I tailored the assignments around how I wanted them to interact with the history of Asian indenture. A student-centered learning approach inspired me to ditch my lectures and focus on research-oriented engagement with historical material. In the first step, students watched a documentary and chose three sources on the history of Asian indenture from a list I provided (see below). The second step asked students to interact with geographic and tabular information from a set of historical data about "coolie" vessels, digitized with Tableau software. In the third step, students synthesized their thoughts in a short research proposal. In what follows, I will describe the materials used in this learning module, detail assignment prompts, and provide examples of student responses. In 2021, I worked with my class to construct material for an eighth-grade social studies inquiry based on this initial pilot. My student, Karen Lau, and I revised and edited this curriculum for the CT Humanities Teach-It Project; this free digital content can be accessed by anyone and is aligned with the middle school College, Career, and Civics (C3) Inquiry Framework.[8]

Comparing Primary Sources

After reading Erika Lee's chapter on Asian indenture, the students were ready to read primary sources to complicate and enrich their understanding. First, I wanted to give students a sense of the scarcity of knowledge on this subject by having them evaluate the types of records and historical evidence created from the "coolie trade." To do so, I assigned the BBC documentary *Coolies: How the British Reinvented Slavery*.[9] This film traces the beginnings of the British indenture system as well as the lives of several descendants of indentured South Asians in Guiana. What is particularly illuminating about the film are the obstacles that the narrators encounter as they attempt to recover their history from lost or deteriorated records and the necessity of traveling across the far-flung geography of the British Empire to track down evidence and speak with elders who survived plantation life in South America. This documentary prepares students to evaluate different types of sources and inquire why certain types of knowledge survives or perishes.

Understanding the scarcity of knowledge about Asian indenture informs students about the relevance of methodology to writing history and helps to build a critical analysis of available historical evidence. In response to the documentary, one student wrote that the film "provides both the emotional and physical firsthand accounts of the abuses in the 'coolie trade,' which can be seen from the woman forced to have her children born into 'coolie' servitude. The fact that this story comes from an individual who has actually lived through the trade is enough justification for how her story and those whose stories are not yet told should be given recognition."

I provided a list of six sources, of which they were to choose three. Since some of these sources are quite long, I asked them to review the table of contents of each and make a fifteen-page selection from each document that most interested them. The students were directed to take independent research notes that included quoted passages of significance, an evaluation of each author's audience and intent, and initial thoughts about similarities and contrasts between sources. This task builds archival research skills as well as teaches varied perspectives on the "coolie trade."

The six sources were President Lincoln's 1861 message on the "Asiatic Coolie Trade"; the log of the "Coolie Master" on the *Forest Eagle* from the same year; Edward Jenkins's 1871 *The Coolie: His Rights and Wrongs*; the 1874 report by the Chinese Commission to Cuba; Don Aldus's 1876 *The Coolie Trade and Kidnapping*; and Watt Stewart's 1951 *Chinese Bondage in*

---

8   Jason Oliver Chang and Karen Lau, "Asian American History in the Civil War Era: Connecticut's Connection to the Trade in Indentured Chinese Workers," Teach It: Bringing Connecticut History to the Classroom, December 14, 2021, https://teachitct.org/lessons/asian-american-history-in-the-civil-war-era-connecticuts-connection-to-the-trade-in-indentured-chinese-workers/.

9   Deep Sehgal, dir., "Coolies: How Britain Reinvented Slavery," produced by BBC Bristol, 2005, video, 58:30, https://www.youtube.com/watch?v=3Cncg3yhWPI.

Peru.[10] The documents range from reports by different governments to firsthand accounts of the Asian indenture trade, interviews with indentured workers, an abolitionist exposé, and historical sociology. Since not all students chose the same three sources, their comparative analyses differed and were insightful for classroom discussion.

Through engagement with these documents, students identified key features of Asian indenture. Of President Lincoln's message, one student wrote, "This collection of documents from Lincoln's time in office does two things for us. It informs us of the role that American ships played in the 'coolie trade' and the maltreatment that occurred aboard the vessels." Another wrote, "This document was important because it provides evidence that 'coolie' traders knew that how they were conducting their business was abusive and illegal and did so for profit." Clues from the testimonies included as addendum to the president's message led another student to observe that "workers were ethnically diverse but were all meshed together. They were unable to communicate but had to work with each other. It was a smart move on the employer's part. If they can't understand each other they would not be able to band together to rebel against their planters." From the *Forest Eagle* log, one student wrote, "This account does a great job of showing how long these voyages actually took. It was roughly four months and twenty-six days that the workers had to survive on this ship." Interpreting Jenkins's book, a student wrote, "It's a valuable source of information about the extent of philanthropic groups that existed in the 1800s who were opposed to the coolie system and actively sought its abolition. . . . The book showed that the 'coolie trade' was a system that many were fighting against, it did not exist unchallenged."

Another student shared the following about the selection of women candidates in India: "The really baffling part of the South Asian indenture trade was the morality testing of these women administered by British colonial officials." The student found it difficult to understand why such high standards were put in place for people who were treated as less than human. Shifting to the indenture experience in Peru, students found Stewart's book to be informative. Such interconnected nuance is reflected in this summary: "This source is especially expedient as it illuminates the hands-off approach of the government. They were informed of the 'coolie' trade's 'Social Evils' and still transferred power to plantation masters who were acquitted from following the law." Another student wrote, "Chinese in

10   United States Department of State, *Message from the President of the United States in Answer to a Resolution of the House of 13th July Last, in Relation to the "Asiatic Coolie Trade"* (Washington: Government Printing Office, 1861), https://archive.org/details/messagefrompresi8121unit; John O. Shaw, "Log of the *Forest Eagle* of Incidents Appertaining to the Emigrants from Macao to Havan, 500 in Number; Rept. by John O. Shaw, Coolie Master" (Searsport, ME: Penobscot Marine Museum, 1861), http://www.penobscotmarinemuseum.org/pbho-1/collection/coolie-masters-logbook; Edward Jenkins, *The Coolie: His Rights and Wrongs* (New York: George Routledge and Sons, 1871), https://archive.org/details/cooliehisrightsw00jenk; China Cuba Commission, *The Cuba Commission Report: A Hidden History of the Chinese in Cuba; The Original English-Language Text of 1876* (Baltimore: John Hopkins University Press, 1993); Don Aldus, *Coolie Traffic and Kidnapping* (London: McCorquodale, 1876), https://archive.org/details/coolietraffican00aldugoog; Watt Stewart, *Chinese Bondage in Peru: A History of the Chinese Coolie in Peru, 1849–1874* (Durham, NC: Duke University Press, 1951), https://archive.org/details/chinesebondagein00stew.

Peru were not punished with typical means, like prisons and fines. Rather they suffered outlandish contract extensions that most certainly were destined to end in death. This document illustrates how disposable the 'coolies' were viewed as and illustrates their subjection to such harsh environments for the sake of profits." These documents offer compelling ethnographic detail and important historical facts that illustrate two important things: the brutal consequences of racism and the conditions of life in the wider diaspora of Asians across the Americas.

Visualizing Asian Indenture Vessels from 1847 to 1874

In the second module, I introduced students to a data story visualizing vessel data from the trade in indentured Asian workers. Data on transport vessels from 1847 to 1874 appears in the appendix of Arnold Meagher's book *The Coolie Trade: The Traffic in Chinese Laborers to Latin America, 1847–1874*.[11] With the help of my research assistant, Orlando Deavila, and technical aid from UConn librarian Steven Batt, I digitized Meagher's tables and assigned other useful information to the data set, like the longitude and latitude of origin and destination ports. For missing information, like the size of the "coolie" cargo, I made calculated guesses to estimate numbers based on the passengers of other similarly sized vessels. With this data set I was able to produce an animated map of the trade as well as graphs of cross-tabulated data. The graphs analyze growth and decline of the international fleet of vessels engaged in the trade as well as the scope of worker-passenger deaths.[12]

After working with these interactive data visualizations, students developed a different understanding of Asian indenture in the nineteenth century. One student wrote, "Analyzing these primary accounts alongside the data visualizations speaks to the scale and frequency of the atrocities described in individual accounts." By reading the data, another student observed that "ship captains stocked their hulls beyond capacity to maximize profits, even if it resulted in loss of life." Another student reflected, "Through this data visualization we get an analytical and emotional portrayal of the so-called 'pig trade.'" These tasks built familiarity with the geography of Asian indenture as well as the scale and intensity of these coerced migrations.

The data story provides a critical supplement to the historical development of the "coolie" and a fascinating context to discuss Asian migrations during the US Civil War. When students were shown graphs illustrating the change in the quantity, destination, and flags of ships from 1847 to 1874, I asked them to tell me a story that explains the changes in the graph. I put special attention on the influence of President Lincoln's ban on US participation in the transportation of indentured Asian workers as well as the impact of the US Civil War on agricultural production in Cuba and Peru (the primary destination of indentured Asian workers in the Americas). This exercise emphasizes interpretive skills for students in the application of the context and understanding established in the first module to the

---

11   Arnold J. Meagher, *The Coolie Trade: The Traffic in Chinese Laborers to Latin America, 1847–1874* (Bloomington, IN: Xlibris Corp, 2008).

12   The map and graphs in this data story are available to view at the following permalink: https://public.tableau.com/app/profile/jason.chang/viz/shared/KD3ZJGNG5.

quantitative analysis of the graphs. When students are able to draw conclusions on their own about the data, based on their understanding of the historiography and primary documents, they create their own connections to Asian American history. This approach encourages creative thinking and thoughtful speculation.

Synthesis

In the third and last module, students were asked to use the materials described above to write a proposal for a research question left unanswered. Students were asked to ground their proposals in the sources by providing quotes from significant passages. They were also required to provide justification for the proposed research by telling why their question is valuable for public knowledge. Students responded with a variety of research proposals. Here is a sample of the more interesting questions: What was the extent of the unregistered trade in indentured Asian workers? How did the price of indentured workers change over time? What happened to the families that indentured workers left behind? What did indentured workers do when they successfully mutinied aboard a ship? How do the descendants of indentured workers think about the history of the "coolie trade"? What was the experience of indentured Chinese workers in Jamaica, a majority Black society? Why did "coolie" transportation become more deadly after President Lincoln's ban on US participation?

In evaluating the proposed research in the context of Asian American history, students identified the need to map a broader geography, account for relationships to slavery, and distinguish between immigration and importation. The writing prompt did provide a useful launching point for discussing the links described by my earlier quote of Erika Lee's introduction to "coolie" history. When students work with diverse source material, they engage with the global structure of the Chinese diaspora in the mid-nineteenth century. As a result, students have a deeper appreciation for Chinese migration to California as a variant of other streams in the diaspora and identify the ways these migrants fit into global economic changes as well as the US postbellum period of racial transformation. When students are familiar with the history of Asian indenture, they will be able to identify the ways that US media accounts stereotype all Asian immigrants as "coolies" or disposable workers. The work of dismantling this stereotype begins with understanding its history.

FROM PLANTATION PERCUSSION TO THE SOUND OF SOLIDARITY: AFRO-ASIAN ECHOES IN THE DRUM SET

BENJAMIN BARSON

The violence of the "coolie" system is both exceptional and part of a larger pattern of racialized labor that powered plantations in the Americas. The abuses and social dislocation foisted upon these workers has been erased from public consciousness. Apologists for slavery and capitalism have attempted to sanitize the barbaric practices of plantation bosses and the commodities they produced. Recovering the historical experience of Chinese laborers in the Americas must be understood to be part of a larger project of redress that can help inform contemporary intersectional movements for antiracism and decolonization. As Édouard Glissant reminds us, "Forgetting offends, and memory, when shared, abolishes this offense."[1] This section of *The Cargo Rebellion* will highlight the ways in which the musical culture of Louisiana serves as a potent repository of remembering, if we choose to hear it.

Chinese workers on Louisiana plantations profoundly shaped the evolution of American music, contributing distinct instruments and percussive techniques to African American musical culture, most notably in the drum set. The drum set was a major development in the history of African American instrumental music, as it reflected the first time a single percussionist could play all the parts of the percussion ensemble. Instead of segregating the low bass drum performer from snare drum and cymbal players, one musician was now responsible for performing each—simultaneously. The instrument revolutionized popular music in the United States and eventually that of the entire world. The performer not only was required to navigate a polyrhythmic practice, but also a polycultural one, for as we will see, the drum set had distinctly Chinese characteristics. African American musicians were inspired by the musical practices of Chinese indentured workers who contracted, married, and showed solidarity with their African American counterparts, and this social history became reflected in the evolution of this incredible instrument. The entangled history of Chinese and African percussion on the plantation adds to the historiography of the "coolie" trade by showing how musical culture enriched the lives of indentured workers and became the substance of interracial encounters, most notably with formerly enslaved African Americans.

---

1   Édouard Glissant, *Une nouvelle région du monde* (Paris: Gallimard, 2006).

From 1867 to 1875, thousands of Chinese laborers were brought into Louisianan plantation districts to weaken the labor power of Black workers, such as it was in the aftermath of the Civil War and the abolition of slavery. John Burnsides, the richest slaveholder and richest planter in antebellum Louisiana, wrote to another planter, Edward J. Gay, that "the Coolie competition will bring n----s to their senses."[2] Burnsides hoped the introduction of indentured Chinese would scare Black laborers into working harder for less. Around the same time, journalist Whitelaw Reid reported that he had heard many Southern whites exclaim, "We can drive the n----s out and import coolies that will work better, at less expense, and relieve us from this cursed impudence."[3] Reid's reporting illustrated that planters and many across the South were only comfortable with nonwhites if they were enslaved, indentured, or unfree in some fashion.

To the dismay of Edward J. Gay, Chinese workers on plantations in Louisiana brought more than their labor. They practiced their culture and found a political solidarity that resonated amongst other communities throughout the sugar parishes. Even though documents are rare, there is no question that the early Chinese immigrant laborers brought their traditional musical culture with them. One piece of evidence for the "rich immigrant musical culture for the early Asian Americans," as Wei-hua Zhang has pointed out,[4] is in the poems carved on the walls of cabins on Angel Island, an immigration station in San Francisco Bay where Chinese laborers were questioned and detained.[5] For contemporary Chinese indentured workers, that was the opera. This folk and refined performance tradition was a popular means of storytelling in southern China, where most Chinese immigrants originated from at the time. The stories of the Cantonese opera told fables, rehearsed local politics, and spoke truth to power. This type of storytelling critiqued authoritarianism and the imperial government, providing a ready-made cultural form for understanding the American plantation. We can turn to an example during this period of indentured Chinese migration to the United States, when the Cantonese opera actor Li Wenmao led an armed uprising during the Taiping Rebellion against the Chinese imperial government in 1854. Performances of Cantonese opera were censored and shut down as a result.[6] The "Red Boat Opera Companies" in central Guangdong province, China, passed on martial arts forms and are speculated by some to have participated in the assassination of

---

2   William Edwards and Co. to Edward J. Gay, September 12, 1867, Edward J. Gray Papers, Louisiana State University; Joseph Karl Menn, *The Large Slaveholders of Louisiana—1860* (New Orleans: Pelican, 1964), 79, 99.

3   Whitelaw Reid, *After the War: A Tour of the Southern States, May 1, 1865, to May 1, 1866*, ed. C. Vann Woodward (1866; reprint, New York: Harper and Row, 1965), 417; Moon-Ho Jung, *Coolies and Cane: Race, Labor, and Sugar in the Age of Emancipation* (Baltimore: John Hopkins University Press, 2006), 79.

4   Wei-hua Zhang, "Fred Wei-han Ho: Case Study of a Chinese-American Creative Musician," *Asian Music* 25, no. 1/2 (1993): 83.

5   Marlon K. Hom, *Songs of Gold Mountain: Cantonese Rhymes from San Francisco Chinatown* (Berkeley: University of California Press, 1987), 72–73.

6   Fred Ho, "Revolutionary Asian American Art," in *Legacy to Liberation: Politics and Culture of Revolutionary Asian Pacific America*, ed. Diane Fujino, Fred Ho, et al. (Edinburgh: AK Press, 2001), 383.

Cantonese opera performers in San Francisco, circa 1900. Chinese opera and popular entertainment have been linked to the martial arts since at least the Song dynasty, and its accompanying musicians were important contributors to an interdisciplinary performance practice. Source: Public domain, previously in the possession of Dr. Benjamin N. Judkins of Kung Fu Tea.

imperial officials.[7] Desperation from political persecution against these hybrid musicians, actors, and storytellers may have led some to choose indenture and migration; others may have been forced into such a fate.

At least some made Louisiana their home. Contemporary newspapers confirmed that musicians were part of the Chinese diaspora who brought these traditions with them. The *Donaldsonville Chief* lamented in 1874 that Chinese laborers had apparently abandoned a plantation. The article reported that they "folded their tents like the Arab, and suddenly stole away. . . . The musical beat of the tom-tom is heard no more in the land."[8] These dismissive remarks leave clues about how the Southern planter class understood the Chinese workers around them. The "tom-tom" mentioned in the report is an important clue to the kinds of instruments Chinese immigrants brought with them or made after their arrival. This tom-tom was likely to have been a *tonggu* drum. This type of drum was used in *Chuida* ensembles, who performed at weddings, funerals, and agricultural ceremonies in

7 Rene Ritchie, *Yuen Kay-San Wing Chun Kuen: History and Foundation* (New York: Multi-Media Books, 1997); Scott Buckler, "The Origins of Wing Chun—An Alternative Perspective," *Journal of Chinese Martial Studies* 6 (Winter 2012): 6–29; Benjamin N. Judkins, "Rethinking Wing Chun's Opera Rebels," Kung Fu Tea: Martial Arts History, Wing Chun and Chinese Martial Studies, September 20, 2018, https://chinesemartialstudies.com/2018/09/20/rethinking-wing-chuns-opera-rebels/.

8 *Donaldsonville Chief*, March 14, 1874; Lucy M. Cohen, *Chinese in the Post–Civil War South: A People without a History* (Baton Rouge: Louisiana State University Press, 1984), 143.

an elaborate, parading fashion that was not dissimilar to New Orleans jazz funerals.[9] The *Opelousas Courier*, by contrast, plays up Chinese music's "discordance," with a revealing comparison of its heterophony to Black musical traditions:

> For discordancy the music of a Chinese orchestra puts Wagner quite in the shade. First one hears wild shrieks, then the thrummings and throbbings as of a thousand negro minstrels, changing to an army of bagpipes, the squealing of maltreated babies, the whistling of loco-motives, the fog horns of a steamer, the clashing of cymbals, the beating of drums. There is a vast assortment of Chinese musical instruments, from the two-stringed fiddle to the great horn. There are three sorts of guitars—the hepa-balloon shaped, three feet in length and much used for festal rites of a religious character; then comes the sanheen or three-stringed guitar, and the full moon guitar, gue kich. There are drums, cymbols [*sic*], etc., and the organ, the embryo of our own, with several tubes of varying length inserted in its bowl.[10]

It is also notable that newspapers from Mississippi, such as Liberty's *Southern Herald*, devoted time to describing Chinese opera. In 1891, one article described them as almost commonplace: "The ordinary Mongolian orchestra, such as is to be found usually dispensing tunes for the delectation of Celestial ears at the Chinese theaters in this city, is composed of ten pieces," and the newspaper even lets its readers know the "bass banjo," probably a *shamisen*, could be obtained for "the sum of two dollars and half" by those who wanted to play such instruments themselves—suggesting adoption beyond the Chinese community.[11]

When we understand that Chinese musicians were present amongst the laborers who were contracted to work on Southern plantations, we can then begin to appreciate the context for hybrid musical forms to emerge. The musical traditions they performed helped weave the social fabric of Chinese communities within the violent and exploitative world of plantation Louisiana. Chinese musical culture reproduced revolutionary, ritualistic, and decidedly working-class performance traditions that had made a lasting impression amongst Afro-Caribbean workers, especially in the sugar parishes, where identity and workplace politics were undergoing radical changes. In eastern Cuba, where sugar production significantly expanded during the second half of the nineteenth century, both *Chuida* ensembles and Cantonese opera introduced a double-reed woodwind instrument known as the *suona*.[12] The instrument became a fundamental part of Afro-Cuban carnival rituals in Santiago de Cuba, revealing intimate contact between these two groups of workers. To this day, Santiago de Cuba's carnival is organized by secret societies known as *oyos*, who spend several months of the year preparing elaborate costumes, extensive choreographies, and

---

9   Peng Xiuwen and Phoebe Hsu, "Chuida Music of Sunan," *Asian Music* 13, no. 2 (1928): 31–38.

10   "A Chinese Orchestra," *Opelousas Courier*, June 19, 1886.

11   "Chinese Orchestras," *Southern Herald*, September 11, 1891.

12   A theater in Cienfuegos, for instance, was described as having a "Chinese orchestra." See Antonio Chuffat Latour, *Apunte Histórico de los Chinos en Cuba* (Havana: Molina, 1927), 43, 39, 57; Lisa Yun, *The Coolie Speaks: Chinese Indentured Laborers and African Slaves in Cuba* (Philadelphia: Temple University Press, 2008), 220.

virtuosic percussion ensembles, in which the *suona*, also known in Spanish as the *corneta china*, is prominently featured.[13] The *suona* is so central to the carnival that experts spend years of their lives practicing for duels with suonaists from other *oyos*, which take place on top of huge parade floats. It is interesting that many so-called "coolie" laborers in Louisiana had initially been contracted in Cuba.[14]

These Spanish-speaking Chinese immigrants moved at an auspicious time. In addition to the complex labor struggles erupting across the sugar parishes, they would find in New Orleans a multigenerational Spanish-speaking community of Africans of Caribbean ancestry who spoke (one of) their language(s). Spanish-speaking Creoles of color would have been able to provide linguistic connections that were not present in other parts of the city. There are clues, both small and large, that the two communities interacted. The jazz clarinetist and Creole of color musician Louis Tio Jr. bought his daughter candy from New Orleans's Chinatown whenever he felt bad about spending too much time out of the house or on the road.[15]

Afro-Caribbean traditions found their way to the US through many ways, but the most important cipher in the nineteenth century was New Orleans. New Orleans's Chinatown was located near Storyville, the city's early-twentieth-century red-light district, which is considered the birthplace of jazz. Evidence of Black and Chinese cohabitation here is verified by the archaeological record, as a saint's medal with Chinese engravings was found in the home of an African American woman, suggesting intermarriage was not uncommon.[16] One African American drummer whose concepts developed in dialogue with the Chinese opera was Abbey "Chinee" Foster, who played in Onward, Excelsior, and several other important brass bands. He was also a friend of Lorenzo Tio Jr. and many other musicians considered key figures in the emergence of jazz. "Chinee is ranked with the all-star great Crescent City drummers," explain the historians Al Rose and Edmond Souchon.[17] In a 1961 interview, Chinee explains that he earned his nickname from playing in a "Chinese act" in a New Orleans theater. Talking about his racial perception amongst New Orleans musicians, he explained:

> Half of them thought I was Mexican, half of them thought I was Spanish, half of them thought I was Puerto Rican. . . . Some of them used to think I was an Indian, like Lorenzo Tio. . . . One time, I went done a show, and done a Chinese Act. So, from then on, white and colored started to call me Chinee. A lot of people were saying, "I'm not calling him Chinee, Chinamen aren't dark like that." And they said, "well, he done that Chinee act, well, good, so, we just call him Chinee." And from that time on, up until now, well, I've been called Mr. Chinee. And very few know of my right name!

---

13 Rolando Pérez Fernández and Santiago Rodríguez González, "La Corneta China (Suona) en Cuba: Una Contribución Cultural Asiática Trascendente," *Afro-Hispanic Review* 21, no. 1 (2008): 139–60.

14 Cohen, *Chinese in the Post–Civil War South*, 143.

15 Rose Wynn Tio, interview with the Hogan Jazz Center, videotape, June 1994.

16 D. Ryan Gray, *Uprooted: Race, Public Housing, and the Archaeology of Four Lost New Orleans Neighborhoods* (Tuscaloosa: University of Alabama Press, 2020), 52.

17 Al Rose and Edmond Souchon, *New Orleans Jazz: A Family Album* (Baton Rouge: Louisiana State University Press, 1967), 43.

It was more than New Orleans's polychromatic universe that led to Foster's nickname. There were lasting resonances from his experience in this mysterious "Chinese Act," which was never discussed by him in detail. Foster refers to his wood blocks as "China Blocks," and he clarifies his crash cymbal was Chinese.[18] It is quite probable that this was a piece of Chinese theater similar to those housed by other cities with Chinese populations in the Caribbean: Cantonese opera.[19] Newspapers of the time, as we have seen, hinted at an extensive Chinese opera scene in the Mississippi Delta region.

It is no coincidence that one of New Orleans's first and greatest drum set players had a connection to Chinese culture. The acclaimed jazz drummer royal hartigan argues that the African American drum set is the result of Chinese and African American cultural collaboration, noting that instruments and playing styles reflect Chinese influence:

> There are many similarities between not only the physical characteristics of Chinese percussion with aspects of the African American drum set, but also in the manner in which individual components are played. For example, the Chinese double hand cymbals (the nao bo) are played by striking up and down (vertically) as opposed to the Western hand-held crash cymbals played striking against each other ("crashing") side to side (horizontally). The high-hat in the drum set is composed of two small cymbals suspended on a pole carriage and played by a foot pedal, clanging vertically. The high-hat, like the nao bo, can be "choked" to create a tightened, nonringing metal accented sound.[20]

In total, the wooden slit blocks, small crash cymbals, temple blocks, high hat, and ornamented tom-tom drums in early drum sets were of Chinese origin, traceable to the Chinese theater productions of the Qing dynasty (1644–1911).[21] Wei-hua Zhang has similarly pointed out how wood blocks used in early drum sets are similar and perhaps traceable to hollow wooden blocks played with a stick in China.[22] Ethnomusicologist Matthew Berger argues that jazz drummers' incorporation of Chinese instruments continued through the first

---

18   Abby "Chinee" Foster, interview with William Russell, March 9, 1961.

19   Many of the Chinese indentured workers in Louisiana had migrated from Cuba. As Ned Sublette notes regarding late-nineteenth-century Havana, "Havana's Chinese community became the largest in the Western Hemisphere, with Chinese banks, newspapers in Chinese, and theaters that played Chinese musicals. In 1875 the Sun Yen, a Chinese opera theater, was inaugurated with Chinese performers from California." Ned Sublette, *Cuba and Its Music: From the First Drums to the Mambo* (Chicago: Chicago Review Press, 2007), 250.

20   royal hartigan, "The American Drum Set: Black Musicians and Chinese Opera along the Mississippi River," in *Afro Asia: Revolutionary Political and Cultural Connections between African Americans and Asian Americans*, ed. Fred Ho and Bill V. Mullen (Durham, NC: Duke University Press, 2008), 289.

21   Matthew R. Berger, "A Cultural History of the Drum Set: Proliferation from New Orleans to Cuba" (master's thesis, Prescott College, 2014), 32; Theodore Dennis Brown, "A History and Analysis of Jazz Drumming to 1942," vols. I and II (PhD diss., University of Michigan, 1976), 48.

22   hartigan, "The American Drum Set," 288.

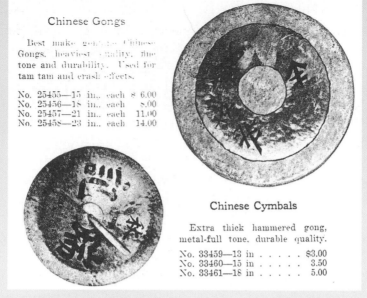

Chinese Gongs

Best make genuine Chinese Gongs. heaviest quality. fine tone and durability. Used for tam tam and crash effects.

No. 25455—15 in.. each $ 6.00
No. 25456—18 in.. each 8.00
No. 25457—21 in.. each 11.00
No. 25458—23 in.. each 14.00

Chinese Cymbals

Extra thick hammered gong, metal-full tone. durable quality.

No. 33459—13 in $3.00
No. 33460—15 in 3.50
No. 33461—18 in 5.00

Photo from an unidentified magazine, circa 1920s. Ragtime and proto-jazz drummers "seem to have favoured these sorts of cymbals almost exclusively during the key developmental period from around 1914–20."
Source: Nicholas D. Ball, "Instruments #8: The Chinese Cymbal, c. 1920s," Drums in the Twenties: Drums, Drummers & Drumming in the 1920s, December 16, 2020, https://drumsinthetwenties.com/2020/12/16/instruments-8-the-chinese-cymbal-c-1920s.

forty years of the twentieth century.[23] Many pictures of early drum sets included gongs, and instrument sellers of the era clearly marketed their products as "Chinese."

When we move beyond instruments themselves to the aesthetics and performance practices of Chinese opera, the picture deepens considerably. The interaction of percussion within the well-developed dramatic form may have resonance with African Americans, hartigan suggests: "In Chinese theater, percussion figures prominently with an array of gongs, cymbals, drums, clappers, and woodblocks that accentuate, highlight, and drive the stage drama. . . . A Chinese opera actor-performer never asks, 'What is my line?' but rather, 'What are my beats?' referring to the percussion rhythms to which they follow and use as a springboard for their particular individual performance."[24] Perhaps this connection between voice and beat influenced drummer Abbey "Chinee" Foster, whose signature musical invention was to use the snare drum to amplify his singing voice.[25] Certainly, this interdisciplinary work spoke to the broad and profound performance traditions already present in New Orleans, from Mardi Gras parades to jazz funerals. It explained why Foster may have not only performed in a Chinese operatic company but also carried the memory of this intercultural collaboration in his very name.

---

23   Berger, "A Cultural History of the Drum Set," 32.

24   royal hartigan, "The American Drum Set," 287.

25   Holly Hobbs, "Sammy Penn—Know Louisiana," 64 Parishes, updated November 30, 2016, https://64parishes.org/entry/sammy-penn.

This photo, tilted "Drummer Plays at Memphis Juke Joint 1930s," features an unknown drummer playing three small Chinese "tack head drums mounted on a big bass drum, as well as a large one to his right. There are two "Chinese" cymbals in this set like the ones marketed in the above ad, with rivets.
Source: Samm Bennett, "Vintage Drum Kits: 1900s–1930s," Polarity Records, https://www.polarityrecords.com/vintage-drum-kits-1900s-through-1930s.html.

Chinese musical creolization with African American culture was certainly not what plantation owners had in mind when they contracted these laborers. Such collaboration was an aesthetic corollary to a larger pattern of Black-Chinese alliances forged during Reconstruction. Consider Tye Kim Orr, "the best-known Chinese who resided in Donaldsonville," who was the director of the town's first school for Black youth. The district's superintendent praised "Mr. Tye Kim Orr" as "one of the best qualified [teachers] in any parish."[26] In 1874, the *Donaldsonville Chief* described him similarly: "Mr. Tye Kim Orr, the Oxford graduate and native of China, resumes control of the Third Ward school

26   William G. Brown, *Annual Report of the State Superintendent of Public Education to the General Assembly of Louisiana for 1875*, 99; Cohen, *Chinese in the Post–Civil War South*, 143.

and the scholars are advancing rapidly under his excellent management."[27] Nine months later, the newspaper doubled down on its praise with the claim that "the schools along the Mississippi river, and that of Mr. Tye Kim Orr on Bayou Lafourche, were never more flourishing and never boasted a larger number of pupils."[28] Mr. Orr seems to have been a complicated figure—he had also helped plantation owners recruit Chinese laborers, even traveling from Louisiana to China to do so—but it is tempting to think that he may have been one of a cadre of English-speaking Chinese teachers working in Black schools.

Historians have noted that Chinese laborers exercised their solidarity with African Americans in other ways, such as by refusing to work altogether.[29] "The Chinese [were not] more amenable to working in a slavelike manner than had been freedmen," surmises John C. Rodrigue, "and they resisted planters' efforts to lower wages and impose discipline. They eventually left the plantations for New Orleans or southern Louisiana's towns."[30] Perhaps their refusal to work was part of the same political philosophy that inspired Orr's work with Reconstruction schools: Chinese immigrants refused to serve as a weapon for white planters against Black labor's bargaining power, even if this meant moving to a yet another adopted home, now with no guarantee of work. Tellingly, the Chinese were seen by progressive commentators as a pillar of New Orleans's unique Reconstruction culture. In 1875, when Louisiana still enjoyed a Reconstruction government that led the nation in desegregation efforts, *Harper's Weekly* explained that New Orleans should never be resegregated, celebrating "the mixture of all shades and colors, including Indians and even Chinese" in the streets of the Crescent City.[31]

In New Orleans, Chinese percussion became foundational to Afro-Atlantic culture at the same time that Black and Chinese laborers exercised their power to negotiate the transition to wage labor and industrialized capitalist social relations. The drum set, a breakthrough in the history of Afrodiasporic music and a foundational instrument in virtually every popular music genre of the twentieth century, reflects how the solidarities in the cane fields and Reconstruction schools became expressed in the musical imagination. As Michael Denning wrote about the vernacular musical forms of the 1920s, "their very noise promised a music beyond the racial orders of colonialism and settler colonialism, a music beyond the commodity forms and labor processes of capitalism: this remains an unfilled promise and unfinished revolution."[32]

These promises to build a better world beyond racial capitalism were encoded in the democratic working-class interculture born in the plantations surrounding New Orleans, manifesting a vibrant dialogue between the Black Atlantic and a Chinese Pacific—an Afro-Asian politics of solidarity—with important lessons for movements against racialized

---

27 *Donaldonsville Chief*, September 26, 1874.

28 *Donaldsonville Chief*, June 5, 1875.

29 Cohen, *Chinese in the Post–Civil War South*, 135.

30 John C. Rodrigue, *Reconstruction in the Cane Fields: From Slavery to Free Labor in Louisiana's Sugar Parishes, 1862–1880* (Baton Rouge: Louisiana State University Press, 2001), 137.

31 "Color in the New Orleans Schools," *Harper's Weekly*, February 13, 1875.

32 Michael Denning, *Noise Uprising: The Audiopolitics of a World Musical Revolution* (New York: Verso, 2015), 233.

violence against Black Americans and Asian Americans today.[33] These mobile workers and their insistence on freedom and creativity in the face of incalculable violence fueled, and fuels, the musical imagination of the modern world.

33 Vijay Prashad, "Bandung Is Done: Passages in AfroAsian Epistemology," in *AfroAsian Encounters: Culture, History, Politics*, ed. Heike Raphael-Hernandez and Shannon Steen (New York: NYU Press, 2006), xi–xxiii; Fred Ho and Bill V. Mullen, eds., *Afro Asia: Revolutionary Political and Cultural Connections between African Americans and Asian Americans* (Durham, NC: Duke University Press, 2008).

WORKS CITED

Bahandur, Gaiutra. *Coolie Woman: The Odyssey of Indenture*. Chicago: University of Chicago Press, 2013.

Ball, Nicholas D. "Instruments #8: The Chinese Cymbal, c. 1920s." Drums in the Twenties: Drums, Drummers & Drumming in the 1920s. December 16, 2020. https://drumsinthetwenties.com/2020/12/16/instruments-8-the-chinese-cymbal-c-1920s/.

Bennett, Samm. "Vintage Drum Kits: 1900s–1930s." Polarity Records. Accessed August 8, 2022. https://www.polarityrecords.com/vintage-drum-kits-1900s-through-1930s.html.

Berger, Matthew R. "A Cultural History of the Drum Set: Proliferation from New Orleans to Cuba." Master's thesis, Prescott College, 2014.

Brown, Theodore Dennis. "A History and Analysis of Jazz Drumming to 1942." PhD diss., University of Michigan, 1976.

Buckler, Scott. "The Origins of Wing Chun—An Alternative Perspective." *Journal of Chinese Martial Studies* 6 (Winter 2012): 6–29.

Chang, Jason Oliver, and Karen Lau. "Asian American History in the Civil War Era: Connecticut's Connection to the Trade in Indentured Chinese Workers." Teach It: Bringing Connecticut History to the Classroom. December 14, 2021. https://teachitct.org/lessons/asian-american-history-in-the-civil-war-era-connecticuts-connection-to-the-trade-in-indentured-chinese-workers/.

Chuffat Latour, Antonio. *Apunte Histórico de los Chinos en Cuba*. Havana: Molina, 1927.

Cohen, Lucy M. *Chinese in the Post–Civil War South: A People without a History*. Baton Rouge: Louisiana State University Press, 1984.

Denning, Michael. *Noise Uprising: The Audiopolitics of a World Musical Revolution*. New York: Verso, 2015.

Glissant, Édouard. *Une nouvelle région du monde*. Paris: Gallimard, 2006.

Gray, D. Ryan. *Uprooted: Race, Public Housing, and the Archaeology of Four Lost New Orleans Neighborhoods*. Tuscaloosa: University of Alabama Press, 2020.

hartigan, royal. "The American Drum Set: Black Musicians and Chinese Opera along the Mississippi River." In *Afro Asia: Revolutionary Political and Cultural Connections between African Americans and Asian Americans*, edited by Fred Ho and Bill V. Mullen. Durham, NC: Duke University Press, 2008.

Ho, Fred. "Revolutionary Asian American Art." In *Legacy to Liberation: Politics and Culture of Revolutionary Asian Pacific America*, edited by Fred Ho, Carolyn Antonio, Diane Fujino, and Steve Yip. San Francisco: AK Press, 2000.

Hobbs, Holly. "Sammy Penn—Know Louisiana." 64 Parishes. Updated November 30, 2016. https://64parishes.org/entry/sammy-penn.

Hom, Marlon K. *Songs of Gold Mountain: Cantonese Rhymes from San Francisco Chinatown*. Berkeley: University of California Press, 1987.

Howland, Douglas, and Luise S. White. *The State of Sovereignty: Territories, Laws, Populations*. Bloomington: Indiana University Press, 2008.

Hu-Dehart, Evelyn. "Chinese Coolie Labor in Cuba in the Nineteenth Century: Free Labor of Neoslavery." *Contributions in Black Studies* 12, no. 5 (1994): 38–54.

Judkins, Benjamin N. "Rethinking Wing Chun's Opera Rebels." Kung Fu Tea: Martial Arts History, Wing Chun and Chinese Martial Studies. September 20, 2018. https://chinesemartialstudies.com/2018/09/20/rethinking-wing-chuns-opera-rebels/.

Jung, Moon-Ho. *Coolies and Cane: Race, Labor, and Sugar in the Age of Emancipation*. Baltimore: John Hopkins University Press, 2009.

Lee, Erika. "Hemispheric Orientalism." *Journal of Asian American Studies* 8, no. 3 (2005): 235–56.

———. *The Making of Asian America: A History*. New York: Simon & Schuster, 2016.

Lopez, Kathleen. *Chinese Cubans: A Transnational History*. Chapel Hill: University of North Carolina Press, 2013.

Menn, Joseph Karl. *The Large Slaveholders of Louisiana—1860*. New Orleans: Pelican, 1964.

Mitsue, Imamura, and Ishimori Kozue. *Yaeyamajin No Shozo*. Ishigaki, Okinawa: Nanzansha, 2004.

Pérez Fernández, Rolando, and Santiago Rodríguez González. "La Corneta China (Suona) en Cuba: Una Contribución Cultural Asiática Trascendente." *Afro-Hispanic Review* 21, no. 1 (2008): 139–60.

Prashad, Vijay. "Bandung Is Done: Passages in AfroAsian Epistemology." In *AfroAsian Encounters: Culture, History, Politics*, edited by Heike Raphael-Hernandez and Shannon Steen, xi–xxiii. New York: NYU Press, 2006.

Ritchie, Rene. *Yuen Kay-San Wing Chun Kuen: History and Foundation*. New York: Multi-Media Books, 1997.

Rodrigue, John C. *Reconstruction in the Cane Fields: From Slavery to Free Labor in Louisiana's Sugar Parishes, 1862–1880*. Baton Rouge: Louisiana State University Press, 2001.

Rose, Al, and Edmond Souchon. *New Orleans Jazz: A Family Album*. Baton Rouge: Louisiana State University Press, 1967.

Sehgal, Deep, dir. "Coolies: How Britain Reinvented Slavery." Produced by BBC Bristol, 2005. Video, 58:30. https://www.youtube.com/watch?v=3Cncg3yhWPI.

Sewall, John S. *The Logbook of the Captain's Clerk*. Edited by Arthur Power Dudden. Chicago: R.R. Donnelley and Sons, 1995.

Siu, Lok. *Memories of a Future Home: Diasporic Citizenship of Chinese in Panama*. Redwood City, CA: Stanford University Press, 2007.

Sublette, Ned. *Cuba and Its Music: From the First Drums to the Mambo*. Chicago: Chicago Review Press, 2007.

Xiuwen, Peng, and Phoebe Hsu. "Chuida Music of Sunan." *Asian Music* 13, no. 2 (1928): 31–38.

Young, Elliot. *Alien Nation: Chinese Migration in the Americas from the Coolie Era through World War II*. Chapel Hill: University of North Carolina Press, 2014.

Yun, Lisa. *The Coolie Speaks: Chinese Indentured Laborers and African Slaves in Cuba*. Philadelphia: Temple University Press, 2008.

Zhang, Wei-hua. "Fred Wei-han Ho: Case Study of a Chinese-American Creative Musician." *Asian Music* 25, no. 1/2 (1993): 81–114.

ABOUT THE CONTRIBUTORS

JASON OLIVER CHANG
Associate professor of history and Asian American
studies at the University of Connecticut and director
of the Asian and Asian American Studies Institute.

BENJAMIN BARSON
Postdoctoral Fulbright Scholar at Instituto de
Investigaciones Culturales–Museo, Universidad Autónoma
de Baja California, baritone saxophonist and composer
who works with the Afro Yaqui Music Collective.

ALEXIS DUDDEN
Professor of history at the University of Connecticut.

ADAM COOPER–TERÁN
Freelance digital producer and media designer for
theater, spectacle, education, and activism.

KIM INTHAVONG
Software engineer and freelance illustrator.
"I would like to thank the CARGO team for all their amazing
work and guidance, my family for making me who I am
today, and finally, special thanks to my friends Diana and
Kristin for their support and feedback throughout."

ABOUT PM PRESS

PM Press is an independent, radical publisher of books and media to educate, entertain, and inspire. Founded in 2007 by a small group of people with decades of publishing, media, and organizing experience, PM Press amplifies the voices of radical authors, artists, and activists. Our aim is to deliver bold political ideas and vital stories to all walks of life and arm the dreamers to demand the impossible. We have sold millions of copies of our books, most often one at a time, face to face. We're old enough to know what we're doing and young enough to know what's at stake. Join us to create a better world.

PM Press
PO Box 23912
Oakland CA 94623
510-703-0327
www.pmpress.org

PM Press in Europe
europe@pmpress.org
www.pmpress.org.uk

FRIENDS OF PM

These are indisputably momentous times—the financial system is melting down globally and the Empire is stumbling. Now more than ever there is a vital need for radical ideas.

In the many years since its founding—and on a mere shoestring—PM Press has risen to the formidable challenge of publishing and distributing knowledge and entertainment for the struggles ahead. With hundreds of releases to date, we have published an impressive and stimulating array of literature, art, music, politics, and culture. Using every available medium, we've succeeded in connecting those hungry for ideas and information to those putting them into practice.

Friends of PM allows you to directly help impact, amplify, and revitalize the discourse and actions of radical writers, filmmakers, and artists. It provides us with a stable foundation from which we can build upon our early successes and provides a much-needed subsidy for the materials that can't necessarily pay their own way. You can help make that happen—and receive every new title automatically delivered to your door once a month—by joining as a Friend of PM Press. And, we'll throw in a free T-shirt when you sign up.

Here are your options:

- $30 a month: Get all books and pamphlets plus 50% discount on all webstore purchases
- $40 a month: Get all PM Press releases (including CDs and DVDs) plus 50% discount on all webstore purchases
- $100 a month: Superstar—Everything plus PM merchandise, free downloads, and 50% discount on all webstore purchases

For those who can't afford $30 or more a month, we have *Sustainer Rates* at $15, $10, and $5. Sustainers get a free PM Press T-shirt and a 50% discount on all purchases from our website.

Your Visa or Mastercard will be billed once a month, until you tell us to stop. Or until our efforts succeed in bringing the revolution around. Or the financial meltdown of Capital makes plastic redundant. Whichever comes first.

The Day the Klan Came to Town
Bill Campbell
Illustrated by Bizhan Khodabandeh
Foreword by P. Djeli Clark

ISBN: 9781629638720 • $15.95

Size: 6x9 • Pages: 128

The year is 1923. The Ku Klux Klan is at the height of its power in the US as membership swells into the millions and they expand beyond their original southern borders. As they continue their campaigns of terror against African Americans, their targets now also include Catholics and Jews, southern and eastern Europeans, all in the name of "white supremacy." Incorporating messages of moral decency, family values, and temperance, the Klan has slapped on a thin veneer of respectability and become a "civic organization," attracting new members, law enforcement, and politicians to their particular brand of white, Anglo-Saxon, and Protestant "Americanism."

Pennsylvania enthusiastically joined that wave. That was when the Grand Dragon of Pennsylvania decided to display the Klan's newfound power in a show of force. He chose a small town outside of Pittsburgh named after Andrew Carnegie, a small, unassuming borough full of Catholics and Jews, the perfect place to teach immigrants a "lesson." Some thirty thousand members of the Klan gathered from as far as Kentucky for "Karnegie Day." After initiating new members, they armed themselves with torches and guns to descend upon the town to show them exactly what Americanism was all about.

The Day the Klan Came to Town is a fictionalized retelling of the riot, focusing on a Sicilian immigrant, Primo Salerno. He is not a leader; he's a man with a troubled past. He was pulled from the sulfur mines of Sicily as a teen to fight in the First World War. Afterward, he became the focus of a local fascist and was forced to emigrate to the United States. He doesn't want to fight but feels that he may have no choice. The entire town needs him—and indeed everybody—to make a stand.

> "A piece of American history in all its ugliness told as an astonishing coming together of misfits to stand up against a common threat. Bill brings an international scope to the history and a concise understanding of politics to the story. Bizhan's art is dazzling. This is a book for our times."
> —Thi Bui, author of *The Best We Could Do*

Maroon Comix: Origins and Destinies
Quincy Saul
Illustrated by Seth Tobocman, Mac McGill, and Songe Riddle

ISBN: 9781629635712 · $15.95

Size: 8.5x11 · Pages: 72

Escaping slavery in the Americas, maroons made miracles in the mountains, summoned new societies in the swamps, and forged new freedoms in the forests. They didn't just escape and steal from plantations—they also planted and harvested polycultures. They not only fought slavery but proved its opposite, and for generations they defended it with blood and brilliance.

Maroon Comix is a fire on the mountain where maroon words and images meet to tell stories together. Stories of escape and homecoming, exile and belonging. Stories that converge on the summits of the human spirit, where the most dreadful degradation is overcome by the most daring dignity. Stories of the damned who consecrate their own salvation.

With selections and citations from the writings of Russell Maroon Shoatz, Herbert Aptheker, C.L.R. James, and many more, accompanied by comics and illustrations from Songe Riddle, Mac McGill, Seth Tobocman, and others, *Maroon Comix* is an invitation to never go back, to join hands and hearts across space and time with the maroons and the mountains that await their return.

> "With bold graphics and urgent prose, *Maroon Comix* provides a powerful antidote to toxic historical narratives. By showing us what was, Quincy Saul and his talented team allow us to see what's possible."
> —James Sturm, author of *The Golem's Mighty Swing*

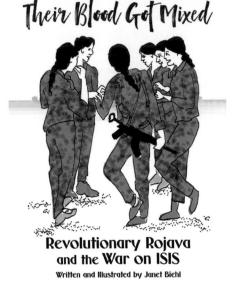

Revolutionary Rojava and the War on ISIS
Written and Illustrated by Janet Biehl

Their Blood Got Mixed: Revolutionary Rojava and the War on ISIS
Janet Biehl
ISBN: 9781629639444 • $27.95
Size: 7x10 • Pages: 256

In the summer of 2012 the Kurdish people of northern Syria set out to create a multiethnic society in the Middle East. Persecuted for much of the 20th century, they dared to try to overcome social fragmentation by affirming social solidarity among all the region's ethnic and religious peoples. As Syria plunged into civil war, the Kurds and their Arab and Assyrian allies established a self-governing polity that was not only multiethnic but democratic. And women were not only permitted but encouraged to participate in all social roles alongside men, including political and military roles.

To implement these goals, Rojava wanted to live in peace with its neighbors. Instead, it soon faced invasion by ISIS, a force that was in every way its opposite. ISIS attacked its neighbors in Iraq and Syria, imposing theocratic, tyrannical, femicidal rule on them. Those who might have resisted fled in terror. But when ISIS attacked the mostly Kurdish city of Kobane and overran much of it, the YPG and YPJ, or people's militias, declined to flee. Instead they resisted, and several countries, seeing their valiant resistance, formed an international coalition to assist them militarily. While the YPG and YPJ fought on the ground, the coalition coordinated airstrikes with them. They liberated village after village and in March 2019 captured ISIS's last territory in Syria.

Around that time, two UK-based filmmakers invited the author to spend a month in Rojava making a film. She accepted, and arrived to explore the society and interview people. During that month, she explored how the revolution had progressed and especially the effects of the war on the society. She found that the war had reinforced social solidarity and welded together the multiethnic, gender-liberated society. As one man in Kobane told her, "Our blood got mixed."

"How to capture history as it is in the making? Janet Biehl's art is a powerful testimony of the dedication, the friendships, dreams, and sacrifices that animate one of the most radical moments in world freedom history. This book is a timely aesthetic company our imagination needs in times of planetary dangers. It is a concrete form of solidarity."
—Dilar Dirik, author of *The Kurdish Women's Movement: History, Theory, Practice*